Office of Government Commerce

For Successful Risk Management:
Think M_o_R®

London: TSO

information & publishing solutions

Published by TSO (The Stationery Office) and available from:

Online
www.tsoshop.co.uk

Mail, Telephone, Fax & E-mail
TSO
PO Box 29, Norwich, NR3 1GN
Telephone orders/General enquiries: 0870 600 5522
Fax orders: 0870 600 5533
E-mail: customer.services@tso.co.uk
Textphone 0870 240 3701

TSO Shops
16 Arthur Street, Belfast BT1 4GD
028 9023 8451 Fax 028 9023 5401
71 Lothian Road, Edinburgh EH3 9AZ
0870 606 5566 Fax 0870 606 5588

TSO@Blackwell and other Accredited Agents

First published 2007

N568991591   c7   12/07

Contents

Foreword

There is an element of risk in almost every activity that we carry out, whether at home, in the office or even walking along the street. But if we set out to avoid all risk then we would never actually do anything. In business, to avoid risk is also to avoid opportunity and that doesn't create a very compelling business model!

What we must do is learn to manage risk in a way that works to our advantage. The Office of Government Commerce's guidance on risk management shows how to make an effective assessment of risk and then manage it accordingly. Rather than stifling business, it creates a confident environment for future development.

I appreciate that risk management may not sound like the most exciting of topics but it is essential if you are to move your business forward. The potential complexity of the subject is overcome in this useful publication. It presents the key elements of management of risk in a well structured, summarized format that will provide a good basic level of understanding for all readers. To not read it is surely a risk in itself!

S. Collier

S Collier
Executive Director
Office of Government Commerce

Acknowledgements

The Office of Government Commerce (OGC) is grateful to the following individuals for their significant contributions under contract to the design and development work in writing the content of this publication: Mike Ward and John Humphries (Outperform UK Ltd).

OGC would also like to thank the following individuals and their organizations for their contributions in reviewing this publication.

REVIEWERS

Anne-Marie Byrne	OGC
Keith Coleman	Quality Liaison Services Ltd
Val Cragg	HM Revenue and Customs
Rubina Faber	Regal Training
John Innes	Avon and Somerset Police
Val Jonas	Risk Decisions
Dominic Kirby	Portsmouth City Council
Russell Macdonald	The Macdonald Craven Partnership Ltd
Tony Marshall	Tay-Mar Consultants
Wendy Mills	The Law Society
Michael Pears	Department for Children, Schools and Families
Stefan Plocki	PSMS Ltd
Tim Reeks	HM Revenue & Customs
Michelle Rowland	A&J Project Management Ltd
Graham Williams	GSW Consultancy
Andrew Wood	Serco Group

Particular thanks go to Jon Akehurst and Kim Watts (EDF Energy), Keith Gray (Business Growth Solutions Ltd), Dusty Miller (Sun Microsystems Inc.), Andy Murray (Outperform UK Ltd), Viciane Beauduin (EFQM), Beth Ackers (International Power PLC) and Andrew Wood (Serco Group) who donated their practical experience to help provide some of the examples.

The OGC would also like to express its gratitude to the Best Practice User Group (BPUG) for coordinating part of the review and to the APM Group for organizing the quality assurance.

Introduction

1

1   Introduction

Is it better to take on risk or avoid it?

Executives ignoring the threats from their competitors run the risk of their organization lagging behind and losing market share, whilst organizations that embrace risk often gain advantage and capitalize on opportunities. *Management of Risk: Guidance for Practitioners* (M_o_R Guidance) provides information about creating an environment for making informed decisions about the risks that affect all of the activities within an organization.

This book is intended as a fast-track introduction to the M_o_R Guidance and has been written to appeal to a wide audience. So, if you are embarking on a new venture or assessing your current situation, or just need to know how to start managing risk then this book is for you. Within this book, the concepts and principles of management of risk (M_o_R) are introduced by using a number of real-life examples; whilst these examples may not exactly follow the M_o_R Guidance, they do illustrate how M_o_R has been applied within that particular organization. This book will help organizations and their executives to develop a more mature approach to dealing with the risks that they face.

Within any organization, the approach to risk management will lie somewhere between:

■ Maintaining the status quo through day-to-day management of the organization's product or service delivery, and
■ Establishing the future direction for the organization and moving the organization in that direction by means of change management.

The M_o_R Guidance describes risk management from four different organizational perspectives: Strategic, Programme, Project and Operational. Each perspective may well require a different approach to risk management along the scale outlined above.

The M_o_R Guidance describes a framework which brings together a set of principles, an approach, a process, and includes advice on where to find further information on risk management techniques and specialisms. It also provides guidance on how to embed risk management into an organization depending on the nature of the organization and the objectives at risk. Figure 1.1 represents the framework.

Figure 1.1 The M_o_R framework

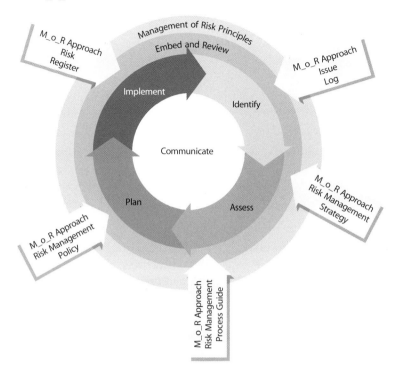

The four core concepts on which the management of risk framework (M_o_R framework) is built are:

- M_o_R principles: these principles are essential for the development of good risk management practice. They are all derived from corporate governance principles in the recognition that risk management is a subset of any organization's internal controls.
- M_o_R approach: the M_o_R principles need to be adapted and adopted to suit each individual organization. Accordingly, an organization's approach to these principles needs to be agreed and defined within a Risk Management Policy, Process Guide and Strategies, and supported by the use of Risk Registers and Issue Logs.
- M_o_R processes: these four main process steps describe the inputs, outputs and activities involved in ensuring that risks are identified, assessed and controlled.
- Embedding and reviewing M_o_R: having put in place the M_o_R principles, approach and processes, an organization needs to ensure that they are consistently applied across the organization and that their application undergoes continual improvement in order for them to be effective.

THE STRUCTURE OF THIS BOOK

Chapter 2 explains the definitions of the key terms used in risk management. Besides describing what risk management is, this chapter describes who is involved in risk management and when it should be done. It also introduces the 12 guiding principles of risk management.

Chapter 3 shows how the management of risk can fit into an organization and explains why it should be adopted.

Chapter 4 explores where threats and opportunities can come from. This is achieved by viewing the organization from the four perspectives: Strategic, Programme, Project and Operational.

Chapter 5 shows how to implement the risk management process by going through each of the process steps, using a number of real-life examples to illustrate some of the key points.

In Appendix A there are outlines of some of the useful management of risk documents which can be used when embarking on a risk management implementation. Other key documents such as the Risk Management Policy, Risk Management Process Guide, Risk Management Strategy, Risk Register and Issue Log are described in the M_o_R Guidance and are therefore not reproduced here.

Appendix B outlines how to perform a risk management healthcheck. This can be used to check the current health of risk management in the organization and identify where the application of risk management might be improved.

Appendix C describes how to conduct a self-assessment in order to benchmark the current risk management maturity level of the organization against the criteria defined by the model.

At the end of the publication, there is a list of further sources of information and a glossary of terms.

What is at risk? 2

2 What is at risk?

In this chapter the definitions of the key terms used in risk management are explained.

RISKS AND OPPORTUNITIES

The M_o_R Guidance defines a risk as 'an uncertain event or set of events that, should it occur, will have an effect on the achievement of objectives'. A risk consists of a combination of the probability of a perceived threat or opportunity occurring and the magnitude of its impact on the objectives.

A threat is an uncertain event that could have a negative impact on objectives or benefits.

An opportunity is an uncertain event that could have a favourable impact on objectives or benefits.

WHAT IS RISK MANAGEMENT?

Risk management is about the systematic application of principles, approaches and processes to the tasks of identifying and assessing risks, and then planning and implementing risk responses. For risk management to be effective, risks needs to be identified, assessed and controlled. This will enable an organization to formulate a response to its vulnerability, and maximize any opportunities that may exist.

WHAT IS A RISK?

It is very easy to start embarking on risk management by listing typical risks that may occur. However, it is worth considering first whether a risk is actually relevant to the activity being undertaken. That is, if the risk materializes, does it have any material effect on the desired outcomes? Risks should be linked to the goals, objectives or expected benefit that an activity will bring. Using this, consider the sequence shown in Figure 2.1.

Figure 2.1 Cause, risk and effect

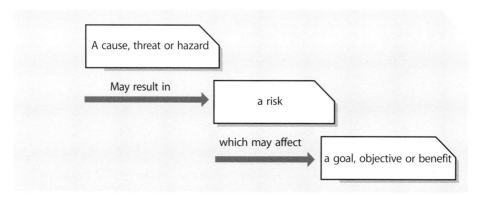

To understand what is potentially at risk, also consider the causes of the risk. What things can lead to this event happening? Understanding this linkage from cause to effect will also assist in identifying the potential individuals who could be responsible for managing that area of risk.

RISK APPETITE

Successful risk takers understand the amount of risk they are prepared to accept – this is called the risk appetite. They also understand their vulnerability in the face of risks and their risk exposure. They operate from a position of power to make informed decisions. Their source of power is knowledge, which comes in the form of answers to a few basic questions such as:

- What objectives or activities are at risk?
- Why are they at risk?
- What is the nature of these risks?
- What are the causes of the risk?

The appetite for risk is specific to an organization and the level at which it is operating. The risk appetite will not be constant and may be influenced by a variety of factors, such as the economic cycle, market maturity and current political situation. Risk appetite at the highest level in the organization is the amount of risk exposure or potential adverse impact from an event that the organization is willing to accept or retain. Organizations that strive towards understanding their risk appetite:

- Provide themselves with a policy for considering and approving levels of risk taking
- Prioritize risk management action by focusing response planning, and monitoring and controlling activities on the risks that can cause the most harm
- Place greater emphasis on risk controls to reduce contingency funds and so achieve a more efficient allocation of capital across the organization
- Better insulate themselves against any shock to future earnings

- Place themselves in a better position to allocate scarce resources and take advantage of beneficial changes in the market
- Leave themselves room for creativity within acceptable limits
- Reduce the possibility of exposure to exceeding capacity due to a lack of awareness
- Make better decisions by changing business direction when it is estimated that attempting to mitigate assessed risks would not bring the risks within acceptable limits.

RISK REGISTER

The Risk Register is where all the information about the risks is stored; it is sometimes referred to as the Risk Log.

RISK PROFILE

The Risk Profile describes the types of risk faced by an organization and its exposure to those risks.

SUMMARY RISK PROFILE

The Summary Risk Profile is a simple mechanism to increase the visibility of risks. It is a graphical representation of information normally found on an existing Risk Register. An example of a Summary Risk Profile can be found in Chapter 5 (section 'Assess – estimate').

RISK TOLERANCE

The risk tolerance is a threshold level of exposure which, when exceeded, will trigger a response, such as reporting the situation to senior management for a decision. Different risk tolerance levels can be set for different areas of the organization and may be set for specific programmes or projects. Benefits of setting a risk tolerance are that:

- Decisions can be made on whether to undertake an activity without prior approval
- It provides an escalation point whereby risks can be referred to a higher level of authority.

M_o_R PRINCIPLES

Although ultimately the risk management processes that are implemented will reflect the business culture which exists in an organization, the M_o_R Guidance offers 12 principles which are high-level, universally applicable guidelines for aiding and influencing the practice of risk management. The principles are derived from proven principles of corporate governance in recognition of the fact that risk management is an integral part of any organization's internal controls. The principles are not intended to be prescriptive, but provide supportive guidance to enable organizations to develop their own policies, process and plans to meet their specific needs. The 12 management of risk principles are:

- Organizational context – a description of the context of the perspective under consideration
- Stakeholder involvement – all major stakeholders must be identified and engaged
- Organizational objectives – acquire knowledge about the objectives
- M_o_R approach – which activities are subject to risk management policies, plans and processes
- Reporting – who needs to know what, in what form and when
- Roles and responsibilities – appropriate support, sponsorship and clarity on who does what
- Support structure – a central risk function should be created
- Early warning indicators – measures of critical business activities
- Review cycle – regular review of effectiveness of risk management policies, plans and processes
- Overcoming barriers to M_o_R – senior management commitment, training, budget, rewards
- Supportive culture – establish culture through management board involvement
- Continual improvement – review practices against a maturity model and plan to progress.

Figure 2.2 The 12 M_o_R principles

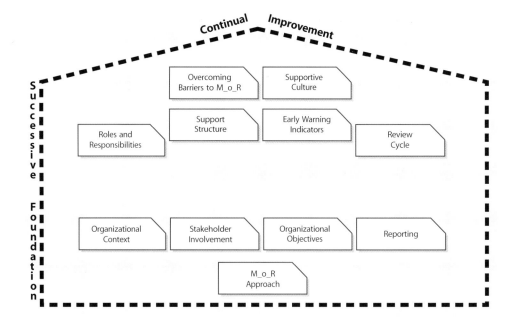

Each of the principles is interdependent (Figure 2.2) and cannot be implemented simultaneously, e.g. some principles have to be in place before the remainder can be established. The principles fall into two categories, foundation and successive: foundation principles need to be established first and have the greatest initial benefit; successive principles provide significant benefits, but on a diminishing scale.

Why M_o_R?
The strategic
context

3

3 Why M_o_R? The strategic context

The main reason for engaging in risk management is to make better, more informed business decisions. A certain amount of risk taking is inevitable if an organization is to achieve its objectives. Organizations that are more risk-aware appreciate that active management of threats and opportunities provides them with a competitive advantage. Taking and managing risk is the very essence of business survival and growth.

BENEFITS OF ADOPTING M_o_R

Before adopting M_o_R, there are a number of questions that need to be answered. What are the benefits of introducing and using M_o_R in your organization, programme or project? Will these benefits outweigh the cost, time and effort that will be required? What are the pros and cons of implementing this new culture?

Effective risk management is likely to improve performance against objectives and provide the following outcomes:

- Being more proactive – looking for potential threats and opportunities and responding to them, leading to fewer surprises
- Increasing focus on doing things right
- More efficient use of resources
- Improving delivery of programmes, projects and services
- Improving process efficiency
- Enhanced safety
- Improving corporate governance, including regulatory compliance
- Enhanced asset management
- Minimizing the potential of legal action
- Improving management of opportunities and innovation
- More responsive to the external environment or market
- More effective business continuity
- Demonstrate knowledge of the business, the risks it faces, and how these risks are managed and controlled.

Some of these benefits can be expressed in hard monetary figures which can be subjected to a financial appraisal. Other benefits are more qualitative in nature but will nevertheless still demonstrate an improvement in the working practices to those involved. However, there may still be a need to 'sell' the ideas of risk management. Some potential 'selling points' are that M_o_R can:

- Increase the probability of success and reduce the probability of failure and the uncertainty of achieving the organization's overall objectives
- Improve decision making, planning and prioritization
- Reduce volatility in the non-essential areas of the business
- Protect and enhance the organization's assets
- Protect and enhance the organization's reputation and brand
- Develop and support people and the organization's knowledge base
- Optimize operational efficiency.

What could possibly be the downside to this? Unfortunately, it takes time, effort and money to develop a risk management framework and to roll it out across the organization; all of this has to happen whilst delivering the current Business Plans.

INTRODUCING M_o_R INTO YOUR ORGANIZATION

Before starting on implementation, find out what already exists in the organization; there may already be procedures and processes, Risk Logs and Risk Progress Reports. Ascertain whether there are any lessons that the organization has already learned about risk. Look for Quality Reviews, audit data, Customer Satisfaction Surveys, End Project Reports and Post Project Evaluation Reports. Consider carrying out a management of risk healthcheck (see Appendix B) to see which risk management principles have been well applied. Also consider using a maturity model to benchmark current capability (see Appendix C). All of this background investigation will help the current risk maturity of the organization to be verified before embarking on an improvement plan.

Implementing M_o_R should be executed as a change programme. It will involve expenditure in developing and producing policies, processes and plans, training, establishing a 'risk-aware' culture, and ongoing support and audit. However, the cost of implementing risk management within an organization is probably much less than the potential costs involved if the organization does not manage risk well. Consider the loss of business revenue, damage to an organization's reputation and credibility, and legal fees and other expenses that are incurred when things go wrong.

The initiative should start with a Business Case which will identify what problems the organization is trying to solve by introducing M_o_R. The Business Case will also highlight the opportunities that could be exploited when it is in place. When developing the Business Case consider how the organization will measure the success of the initiative through its key performance indicators. Will any tangible, quantitative data be available, such as cost savings or reduced incident counts, in addition to the intangible and more qualitative measures, such as providing a healthier work/life balance and improving the risk perception of the organization as seen by its customers and the community it serves?

BARRIERS TO ADOPTING M_o_R

If M_o_R is such a good thing to do, then why are so many obstacles put in place when implementing it? Sometimes there will be a range of negative statements:

- 'We're too risk-averse.'
- 'This is not the way we do it here.'
- 'Senior management doesn't have the time for this.'
- 'It's a bureaucratic nightmare.'
- 'There is no demonstrable value.'
- 'You haven't shown me how to do this.'
- 'Where are the tools to help me?'

To overcome these barriers, the initiative to implement M_o_R must be owned and supported by senior management. Senior managers must apply the principles of good risk management themselves if they want others to follow. The following solution goals must be considered as part of the planning process:

- An organizational culture that understands and values the benefits of risk management
- Agreed risk management practices
- Dedicated risk facilitation, resources and time
- Published risk policies, processes and plans
- A risk management champion
- Education, training and awareness of risk management
- Formal tools and techniques
- Clear guidance for all
- Incentivization for participation in risk management.

WHO SHOULD BE INVOLVED IN MANAGING RISK?

The simple answer is that everyone should be involved in the management of risk in an organization. The M_o_R Guidance identifies the following roles of those people who should be involved in developing and embedding the management of risk culture into an organization and reviewing management of risk within the organization:

- Accounting Officer (or Chief Executive Officer) – acts as the figurehead for the management of risk within the organization. Sometimes referred to as the Risk Director
- Risk Manager (or Risk Improvement Manager) – responsible for ensuring that the M_o_R framework is implemented, managed and improved
- Programme Board, Project Board, operational unit management board, Senior Responsible Owner (SRO) – ensure that they understand their accountability for the process, and manage and escalate risks associated with their areas
- Risk Specialists – responsible for the preparation of Risk Management Strategies, qualitative and quantitative risk analysis, and the production of Risk Progress Reports

- Internal Audit Department – responsible for the formal assessment of risk implementation by implementing a risk healthcheck and assessing whether the appropriate controls are in place to manage risks
- Managers across the organization – responsible for managing risk controls within their areas and promoting risk management principles to their staff
- All staff – responsible for identifying, reporting and escalating risks to management.

A RACI diagram (see Table 3.1) can be used to describe the roles and responsibilities for each of the participants in risk management in an organization. RACI is an acronym formed from the four participatory roles that it describes:

- Responsible – those who undertake the activity
- Accountable – those who take credit for success or failure
- Consulted – those whose opinions are sought
- Informed – those who are kept up-to-date on progress.

Table 3.1 Example RACI Diagram

Item	Responsible	Accountable	Consulted	Informed
Risk Management Policy	Risk Director	The Board	Regulatory Authority	All senior management
Risk Management Process Guide	Corporate Risk Manager	Risk Director	Project Office Manager	Project Managers, Programme Managers
Corporate Risk Register	Corporate Risk Manager	Risk Director	Operations Managers	The Board
Project Risk Register	Project Manager	Project Executive	Corporate Risk Manager	Project Team
Etc.				

Why should risk management be embedded and made part of everyone's job rather than just an add-on for specific undertakings? If M_o_R is an add-on or an optional extra then it is easier to come up with reasons for **not** taking the time to do it. However, if situations are always dealt with in a particular way, the practice becomes second nature; you never forget how to ride a bike. So, if M_o_R becomes the way things are done in the organization then the benefits it can offer can be reaped: the core values of the organization will be strengthened, and stakeholders' confidence in the organization's ability to cope with and manage risks will be enhanced.

WHEN SHOULD RISK MANAGEMENT ACTIVITIES BE UNDERTAKEN?

There are certain times when there should be greater focus on risk management, such as:

- At least annually at the strategic level
- When starting an initiative, programme, project or new service delivery
- When forecasting and planning
- At times of change, such as when reorganizing or relocating
- In the event of incidents or serious events.

When risk management is an established culture in the organization, due care and attention will be applied to risk management in everything that is undertaken and at all times!

ARE THERE ANY TOOLS AVAILABLE TO HELP?

There are over 100 commercially available risk management tools on the market today. So the answer to the question is clearly 'yes', there are tools available. However, will they help? The answer to this question is 'maybe'. It may be prudent to understand the risk management process before embarking on a purchase or development of a tool which might be used to automate the process.

Also, it would be worth finding out what tools people in the organization are already using to capture, analyse and report on risk. Is there a standard Risk Register or Risk Log? Has there been any investment in any specific risk management tools in some part of the organization, and what is the experience of using them?

Further details are provided in M_o_R Guidance, Appendix F: Selecting risk management software tools.

Where does risk come from? 4

4 Where does risk come from?

Businesses and organizations operate in a world full of uncertainties; to compartmentalize them would be helpful to their understanding. The M_o_R Guidance views organizational risk from four different perspectives:

- Strategic – coping with disasters (business continuity), employee/customer satisfaction, managing the media, predicting cash-flow, fluctuation in pricing/exchange/interest rates, credit, fraud, intellectual property, competition, customer demand etc.
- Programme – making sure that the benefits will be realized
- Project – avoidance of being late, over-budget, or failing to meet quality standards
- Operational – compliance with regulations, security, managing hazards/incidents, data protection, health and safety, contracts, culture, employees, property, products and services etc.

Figure 4.1 Inter-relationships between risks 'flowing' between different organizational perspectives

It should be noted from Figure 4.1 that the programme and project risks are solely to do with achieving the objectives of change management, whereas operational risks are concerned with the day-to-day management objectives. Strategic risks must look across both change management and day-to-day management in order to form a complete picture of the organization.

The M_o_R Guidance provides an explanation of how risk management should be applied from each of these perspectives and what to consider when producing the relevant Risk Management Policy. In this chapter the organizational context of each perspective is defined by way of an example, and an overview of the contents of the Risk Management Policy is provided.

Many companies also employ Risk Managers in specific risk management specialisms. Whilst these specialisms are extremely important, they are beyond the scope of this book, and are covered only briefly in the M_o_R Guidance. The specialisms include:

- Business continuity
- Incident (crisis) management
- Health and safety
- Security
- Financial risk management.

STRATEGIC PERSPECTIVE

Strategic risks are risks concerned with ensuring overall business success, vitality and viability. Materialization of strategic risk will be perceivable externally by owners, investors or funders, and will affect the reputation of an organization.

Strategic opportunities and threats are generally identified:

- Through escalation of risks from programme, project or operational activities
- As a by-product of corporate and business planning activities
- By partner organizations that share interests with the organization.

Example

A good place to start in any organization would be to review the Business Plan. The Business Plan will include business objectives and a strategy for key business areas such as operations, finance and human resources. It is also where the ambitions of the organization are likely to be presented as core values.

PEST is a commonly used tool for thinking about factors that may affect the goals, objectives and benefits that you are trying to achieve:

- **P**olitical factors such as tax policy, employment laws, environmental regulations, trade restrictions and tariffs, and political stability
- **E**conomic factors are the economic growth, interest rates, exchange rates and inflation rate
- **S**ocial factors often look at the cultural aspects and include health consciousness, population growth rate, age distribution, career attitudes and emphasis on safety

■ **T**echnological factors looks at elements such as research and development activity, automation, technology incentives and the rate of technological change. Factors may also include ecological and environmental aspects, and can determine the barriers to entry and minimum efficient production level, and influence decisions on outsourcing.

There are many variations to this tool by adding items such as Legal and Environmental (acronym PESTLE).

EDF Energy, one of the largest energy companies in the UK, uses a 'Risk Universe' to describe its strategic and operational perspectives. Table 4.1 shows the areas of risk that the company might encounter in three main areas: the risks which may be encountered from the general environment in which it operates, the operational risks and the strategic and steering risks.

PROGRAMME PERSPECTIVE

Programme risks are those risks concerned with transforming business strategy into new ways of working that deliver measurable benefits to the organization. Stakeholders with an interest in the programme benefits will become aware of the appearance of programme risks.

Programme opportunities and threats are generally identified:

■ Through the escalation of risks from projects within the programme
■ During programme start-up
■ By other programmes with dependencies or interdependencies with this programme
■ By operational units affected by the programme.

Example

The best place to start when trying to understand the context of the programme perspective is the Programme Brief or Programme Definition. The key information that should be included is:

■ Vision Statement – defining the end goal of the programme
■ Benefits Plan – overall schedule for monitoring when benefits are expected to be realized
■ Risk Management Strategy – defining how risks will be identified, assessed and monitored during the programme
■ Risk Register or Log – capturing all identified programme risks.

The context for a programme will fit into one of the areas shown in Figure 4.2. The matrix of programme focus and programme nature is used to characterize a specific programme so that the organization can maintain a view of each of the programmes in its portfolio. The words describing the programme apply to all areas in the box in the figure, but the main focus area of the programme is shaded.

Table 4.1 EDF Energy 'Risk Universe'

EXTERNAL ENVIRONMENT RISKS				
Institutions and society		**Markets**	**Disaster**	
Political Legislation/ regulation	Sensitivity to the general economic context	Price of energy (wholesale markets)	Competition	Natural disaster
			Customer demand	Accident/attack
Market regulation Shareholders	Social and public opinion change	Price of emission permits	Counterparty	
	Positions of stakeholders	Interest rates	Technological change	
		Exchange rates		

OPERATIONAL RISKS		
Transverse	**Human resources**	**Finance**
Efficiency of the organization	People management	Capital
Legal and regulatory compliance	Skills management	Level of debt
Ethics, corporate social responsibility and sustainable development	Change management	Asset value
Core business	Health and safety	Liquidity – free cash flow
Transactions on energy market/ upstream-downstream optimization	Incentives	Financial commitments
Commercial	Integrity	Operations on the financial markets
Billing/revenue collection	Staff satisfaction	Financial credibility
Technical		**Other support processes**
Nature or human environmental damage		External communication
Project management		Information system Procurement – purchasing – suppliers Technological innovation

STRATEGY AND STEERING	
Strategy	**Managing performance**
Business model/process of strategic decision-making	Monitoring performance
Means of governance/strategic implementation	Unknown contractual commitments
Mergers and acquisitions	Control of shares and participations
Partnership management/joint venture	

Figure 4.2 Programme management context

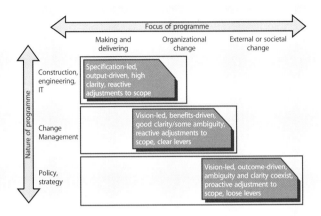

PROJECT PERSPECTIVE

Project risks are those risks concerned with delivering defined outputs to an appropriate level of quality within agreed time, cost and scope constraints. The recipients of project outputs will identify the appearance of project risks that will affect the time, cost, quality or scope of outputs.

Project opportunities and threats are generally identified:

- Through the escalation of risks identified when delivering work packages
- During project initiation
- By other projects within a common programme or other projects within the organization
- By the project's customers and suppliers.

Example

To understand the context of a project, start with the Project Brief and Project Initiation Document. The key information that should be included is:

- Project Definition – explaining what the project needs to achieve
- Business Case – explaining why the project is being undertaken
- Project Plan – detailing any constraints.

The context for understanding the project environment can be understood more easily by having some rules for determining that context. A global IT company developed a very simple set of rules for bid managers responsible for pre-sale proposal writing. The 'Mandatory-6 Rule-set' (Table 4.2) was created to inform a bid manager that if any one of the triggers were true, the proposal had to be reviewed by the senior management team prior to sending it to the customer, since it was determined to be of high risk.

Table 4.2 A global IT company's 'Mandatory-6' triggers

Mandatory-6 Rule-set	Interpretation
Cross-'country'	Solution will need to be developed in more than one country
Discount levels	Standard discount will be exceeded
Mission critical	Solution will be used in a mission-critical environment
Non-standard contract	Special contract terms are required
Non-price listed	The solution is not listed in the sales book
Unreleased product	The solution uses products that have not been approved for general release

OPERATIONAL PERSPECTIVE

Operational risks are those concerned with maintaining an appropriate level of business service to existing and new customers. Customers receiving the affected business service will recognize the appearance of operational risks.

Operational opportunities and threats are generally identified:

- Through the escalation of risks from business or service delivery teams (for example, engineering, information systems, finance, human resources, security, fraud, customer support)
- By service-enabling suppliers
- By service-receiving customers.

Example

Defining the areas of uncertainty within the operational perspective can be difficult. The structure of the organization will show a natural breakdown of responsibilities by functional area; this might be a good place to start to indicate where risks could be managed. A very simple breakdown would be:

- Sales and marketing
- Operations
- Product development
- Finance
- Technology and facilities
- Human resources
- Health and safety.

Consider also taking a cross-functional view of the organization such as:

■ Service/product – failure to deliver the service to the user within agreed/set terms; project delivery – repeated failure to deliver on time/budget/specification

■ Resources – insufficient staff capacity/skills/recruitment and retention; relationships – level of customer satisfaction with delivery; operations – insufficient capability to deliver; reputation – level of confidence and trust in the organization

■ Governance – regularity and agreed processes

■ Resilience – disaster recovery and contingency planning

■ Security of physical assets and of information.

Also consider using a predefined balanced score-card, such as the European Foundation for Quality Management's EFQM Excellence Model® (Figure 4.3). This model is a framework to help organizations to identify areas for improvement in their operations; the model clearly identifies nine areas of focus where risks could be considered. The Risk Support Team at HM Treasury has produced a Risk Management Assessment Framework based on the EFQM Excellence Model. The framework is a tool for assessing the standard of risk management in an organization.

Figure 4.3 EFQM Excellence Model®[1]

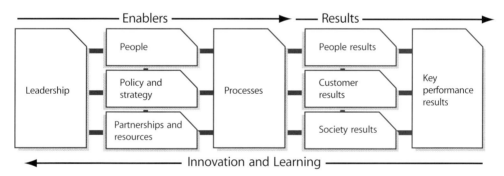

DEVELOPING A RISK MANAGEMENT POLICY

To guide staff on how risk management will be implemented throughout the organization, a Risk Management Policy should be formulated. A Risk Management Policy can be created for the organization as a whole; or a number of policies can be developed – one for each perspective. If there are a number of policies, then the strategic policy drives the policies for the other perspectives (Figure 4.4).

The policy should be concise, easy to read and understandable. Nominated individuals for management of risk roles should be listed in each of the policies when they have understood and accepted the responsibilities that go with those roles. The roles are outlined in Chapter 3 (see section 'Who should be involved in managing risk?').

1   The EFQM Excellence Model is a registered trademark.

Figure 4.4 Inter-relationships between policies at different organizational perspectives

The Management of Risk Policy should cover the following areas:

■ Context of the policy – what is at risk and where are the uncertainties?
■ Benefits – stakeholders want to know what is in it for them
■ Risk appetite and capacity – what level of risk is acceptable and how much risk can we take on?
■ Risk tolerance thresholds – what level of risk needs to be escalated?
■ Procedures for escalating risk – when, how and to whom do risks get escalated?
■ Roles and responsibilities – in relation to management of risk
■ Definitions of special terms – a glossary may be required for consistency of understanding
■ Risk management process – what are the steps?
■ Early warning indicators – are there signs that a risk is becoming more likely to occur?
■ Tools and techniques used – what and how are these used?
■ When risk management should be performed – are there significant times for this?
■ Reporting requirements – who needs to know what, and when?
■ Budgeting for management of risk – what funding needs to be set aside?
■ How will quality be assessed – what are the criteria, quality methods and assessment skills needed?
■ Measuring the benefits – when will the management of risk effectiveness review occur?
■ Related policies – links to other specialist risk areas.

How to apply risk management

5

5 How to apply risk management

There are four primary steps in the risk management process, two of which are broken down into two further steps, namely:

- Identify:
  - Context – gain information about the activity
  - Identify the Risks – identify the risks to achieving objectives
- Assess:
  - Estimate – assess the threats and opportunities
  - Evaluate – understand the net effect of all the risks
- Plan – prepare responses
- Implement – check that the actions are having the desired effect.

Key to the successful implementation of M_o_R is an activity called Communicate, which is carried out throughout the whole process. The overall picture of the M_o_R process is presented in Figure 5.1, along with a list of inputs to each process step. The outputs from each process step form the inputs to the following step. The output from the Implement step is a Risk Progress Report.

Figure 5.1 Management of risk process

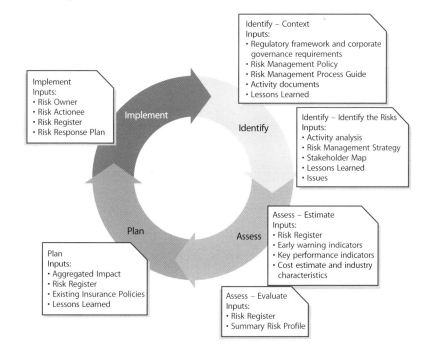

Implement
Inputs:
• Risk Owner
• Risk Actionee
• Risk Register
• Risk Response Plan

Identify – Context
Inputs:
• Regulatory framework and corporate governance requirements
• Risk Management Policy
• Risk Management Process Guide
• Activity documents
• Lessons Learned

Identify – Identify the Risks
Inputs:
• Activity analysis
• Risk Management Strategy
• Stakeholder Map
• Lessons Learned
• Issues

Assess – Estimate
Inputs:
• Risk Register
• Early warning indicators
• Key performance indicators
• Cost estimate and industry characteristics

Plan
Inputs:
• Aggregated Impact
• Risk Register
• Existing Insurance Policies
• Lessons Learned

Assess – Evaluate
Inputs:
• Risk Register
• Summary Risk Profile

Implement

Identify

Plan

Assess

Management of risk is a continual process, with each of the steps being executed many times and not necessarily following one another. Whilst Figure 5.1 conveys a cyclic message (e.g. evaluate before you plan), do not be fooled into thinking that as you go through the steps there will be no more risks to identify.

IDENTIFY – CONTEXT

The first task in the Identify step is to set the context (Context step).

What is the purpose?

The primary goal of the Context step is to obtain information about the planned activity. This includes an understanding of:

- The objectives of the activity
- The scope of the activity
- What assumptions have been made
- How complete the information is
- Who the stakeholders are and what their objectives are
- Where the activity fits in relation to the organizational structure
- The organization's environment (industry, markets, products and services etc.)
- The organization's approach to risk management.

The context setting for any activity may be derived from external items, such as the regulatory framework and corporate governance requirements; and internal items, such as the Risk Management Policy, a Risk Management Process Guide, activity descriptions and lessons learned from previous activities. The inputs required to set the context of the particular activity being undertaken are influenced by the perspective from which the activity is viewed, for example:

- Strategic – market, competition, barriers to market entry, dominance of suppliers, life expectancy of market, projected income, time and cost of entry to market
- Programme – objectives, stakeholders, interdependencies, contributing projects, projected benefits
- Project – objectives, deliverables, project documentation, stakeholders, cost plan, quality plan, approvals, change control process
- Operational – purpose of operation, interfaces, sequences of activities, interdependencies, IT, equipment.

The Context process is described graphically in Figure 5.2.

Figure 5.2 The Context process definition and information flows

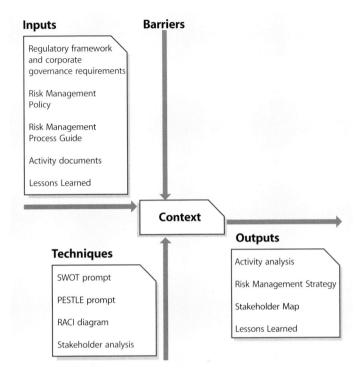

What are the benefits?

The benefits which flow from getting context-related information include:

- Agreement on the organization's approach to risk management
- Improved communications between stakeholders
- A shared understanding of what is to be achieved, how it will be achieved, and when it is required.

Do I have to do this?

Yes, to ensure that there is an appreciation of the context in which risks are to be identified. Knowledge of the context of the planned activity will assist in the creation of informed questions during the Identify the Risks step.

What happens if I don't do this?

If the wider context within which the organization operates is not well understood, then a complete understanding of the threats and opportunities it faces will be difficult to achieve.

How do I do this?

Developing an understanding of the context is aided by the use of techniques such as:

- Project lifecycle – map the activities within a project to the agreed lifecycle of a project to identify potential sources of risk with each activity.
- Process map – using process diagrams, describe the vital steps in the business process. There are many different ways to map a process, such as flow charts and swim-lane diagrams.
- PEST prompt – acronym for Political, Economic, Social and Technological factors. It is a simple tool for helping uncover external risk exposure (and can be extended to consider additional factors such as Legislative, Environmental, Cultural and Industry factors).
- SWOT analysis – acronym for Strengths, Weaknesses, Opportunities and Threats. To use this technique, look at strengths and weaknesses of the organization in the marketplace, and then ask two questions: (1) Considering these strengths, what are the opportunities? (2) Considering these weaknesses, what are the threats?
- RACI diagram – acronym for Responsible, Accountable, Consulted and Informed. It is used to describe roles and responsibilities of the participants in a business or project activity (see Table 3.1).
- Stakeholder matrix – a diagrammatic way to represent the results of a stakeholder analysis.

It is also important to identify the key stakeholders, their respective roles and degree of participation, issues that concern them, and their attitude and interests towards the objectives of the associated activities. Following a stakeholder analysis, the data obtained can be presented using a stakeholder matrix (see Figure 5.3). All of this information should be documented in a Stakeholder Map.

How do I get to the next step in the process?

The outputs needed to proceed to the next step are:

- Activity analysis – from the relevant perspective, using some of the techniques above.
- Risk Management Strategy – how risk management will be performed. Much of this should be derived from the Risk Management Policy and Process Guides.
- Stakeholder Map – who is affected by/affects the activity, and what their related interests are. It can also be useful to establish the degree of power and influence stakeholders have over the life of the activity.
- Lessons Learned – can any learning be derived from previous activities which can feed the next step?

What questions should I ask to get to the next step?

Consider the following:

- Is there anything preventing the process from moving forwards?
- Have the appropriate outputs been created and approved?
- Is there sufficient clarity in the context to enable the threats and opportunities to be identified in the next step?

Are there any examples that might help me?

Figure 5.3 shows an example stakeholder matrix, using what is called a power impact matrix. Note that each band describes the action which must be taken with stakeholders who fall into this category.

Figure 5.3 Power impact matrix

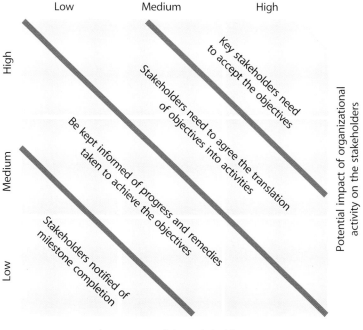

EDF Energy has mapped its operational risk reporting process using a diagram (see Figure 5.4). This diagram shows the activity of the key stakeholders in the execution of the process. Note that this process has a number of outputs, namely an updated Risk Database (labelled RA1), an EDF Energy Risk Report (labelled E6) for internal use, and an EDF Energy Risk Report (labelled P2) which is sent to the parent company, EDF, in Paris.

Figure 5.4 EDF Energy Risk Reporting Process

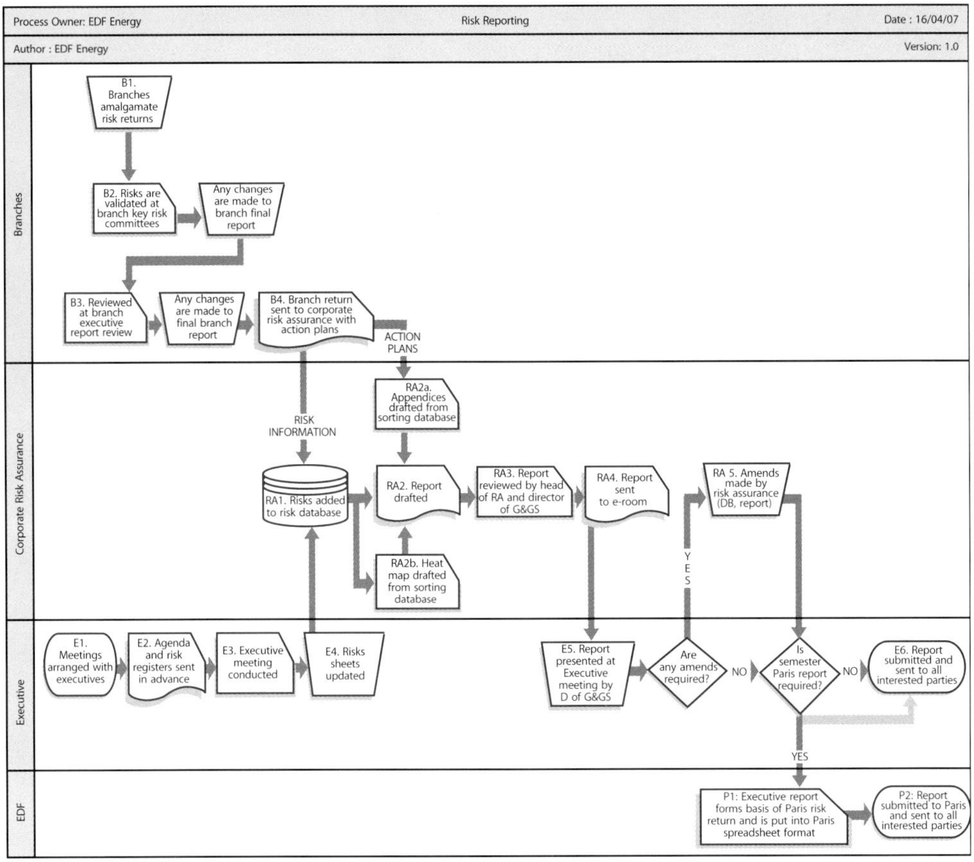

Process Owner: EDF Energy	Risk Reporting	Date : 16/04/07
Author : EDF Energy		Version: 1.0

IDENTIFY – IDENTIFY THE RISKS

The second task in the Identify step is to identify the risks.

What is the purpose?

The primary goal of the Identify the Risks step is to identify the risks to the organization that would reduce or remove the likelihood of the organization reaching its objectives while maximizing the opportunities that could lead to improved performance. This will include:

- Identifying the threats and opportunities to objectives and activities
- Preparing a Risk Register
- Preparing key performance indicators
- Understanding the stakeholders' view of the risks.

The Identify the Risks process is described graphically in Figure 5.5. The inputs to this process step correspond to the outputs of the Context step, along with any additional identified issues.

Figure 5.5 The Identify the Risks process definition and information flows

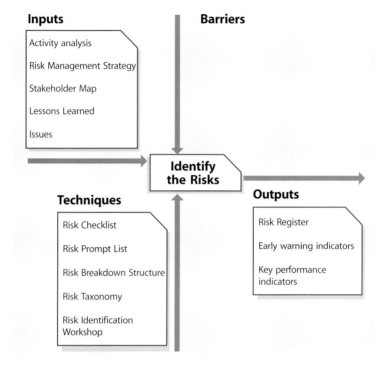

What are the benefits?

Identifying risks is the first step in understanding what can cause the organization to fail to reach its objectives or capitalize on potential opportunities.

When thinking about risks, also try to do root cause analysis to explain the consequences of a simple action:

> For want of a nail the shoe was lost.
> For want of a shoe the horse was lost.
> For want of a horse the rider was lost.
> For want of a rider the battle was lost.
> For want of a battle the kingdom was lost.
> And all for the want of a horseshoe nail.
> *Confessio Amantis*, John Gower, c.1390

Recalling the diagram in Figure 2.1 and slightly modifying it may help to understand the factors that contribute to a risk occurring, and builds up a picture of what can affect the objectives of the activity being undertaken.

Figure 5.6 Cause, risk and effect

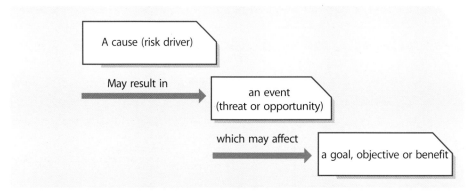

When articulating risks, the following syntax can be useful: due to ... *a cause* ... there is a risk that ... *a threat may occur, which affects the stated objective.*

To put some real words into that structure: due to conflicting demands for specialist resources there is a risk that resources will not be available to start the proposed development, which may delay the introduction of the new payroll system.

Opportunities can be expressed in a similar way: due to ... *a cause* ... there is a risk that ... *an opportunity may occur, which affects the stated objective.*

For example: 'due to good weather, there is a risk that more customers than expected will turn up, which will allow more goods to be sold'.

Do I have to do this?

Yes, to ensure that appropriate risks are identified, to focus people's attention on the uncertainties and potentially harmful risks, along with identification of beneficial opportunities. Risk is not just about 'bad things happening' (the threat), it is also about 'good things not happening' (the missed opportunity).

What happens if I don't do this?

Failing to identify the risks does not mean that they will not happen. However, once they have been identified, a plan can be put in place to deal with them.

If a risk does occur that has not been identified, then a reactive unplanned situation has to be dealt with, with little background knowledge being available. This will almost always lead to increased costs, time delays and a negative effect on morale.

How do I do this?

It is essential to bear in mind the definition of a risk as an uncertain event or set of events that, should it occur, will have an effect on the achievement of objectives.

Risks can be identified by using a variety of techniques such as:

- Project Profile Model – a tool used to identify typical problem areas and criticality to an organization in terms of the scale of a project against central criteria
- Risk Checklist – a list of risks that have been identified during previous organizational activities
- Risk Prompt List – categorizes risks into types and is used for stimulating ideas
- Lessons Learned logs – documented learning from previous activities
- Risk Breakdown Structure – hierarchical decomposition of the activity's environment to help identify potential sources of risk
- Risk taxonomy – a structured checklist that organizes known enterprise risks into a specific hierarchy
- Risk identification workshop – a group session focusing on the identification of risks
- Cause and effect diagrams – to find risk causes and their potential effects (risk effects), often generated diagrammatically in a group session
- Brainstorming – redefining the problem and generating ideas
- Nominal group technique – a form of structured brainstorming
- Delphi technique – a method for the systematic collection and collation of judgements from isolated anonymous respondents on a particular topic
- Risk questionnaire – a tool used to elicit unresolved issues, concerns and uncertainties through a series of questions defined by the needs of the situation
- Risk database – allows risk information to be captured in a controlled and consistent way, and provides the means to communicate risks via reports
- Gap analysis – used to help identify the main risks to an activity; consider using the output of the risk maturity model to focus on areas for improvement.

The justification for an activity will be found in its Business Case. This should identify the organization's business environment and the highest-level areas of risk.

M_o_R Guidance, Appendix C: Management of risk healthcheck, provides useful sets of questions which cover all aspects of the 12 M_o_R principles. These questions also contribute to the Identify process by assisting in teasing out risks.

Risks are recorded in a Risk Register. This is created as part of this process and is a living, evolving document. The contents of the Risk Register will be refined, reviewed and updated as the activity proceeds. A Risk Register can be built using a suitable tool such as a word processor, spreadsheet, database or dedicated software.

Ensure that early warning indicators have been considered and set for the activity. These relate to targets set to measure achievement of an objective and provide measures of a system; as part of the risk identification process, investigate the signs which may indicate that all is, or is not, well. For example, team attendance at weekly meetings, continued funding for the activity, milestones being missed, and communications with suppliers taking place as planned.

Choose appropriate key performance indicators. For example, if services are being provided to end customers, a likely key performance indicator will be 'customer satisfaction'. This key performance indicator is often measured through surveys. Note, however, that it might be easier to collect early warning indicators such as 'customer minutes lost' or 'customer interruptions' which will have a direct effect on the key performance indicator.

How do I get to the next step in the process?

The outputs needed to proceed to the next step are:

- Risk Register – a record of all identified risks relating to an initiative or activity
- Early warning indicators – vital signs or levels which indicate that a risk is becoming more likely and/or its impact is increasing
- Key performance indicators – relate to targets set to measure achievement of objectives.

What questions should I ask to get to the next step?

- Have the available techniques been used to identify the risks?
- Have the potential risks to the activities been recorded in the Risk Register?
- Are the risks sufficiently well articulated to enable them to be subjected to further investigation?
- Have all of the senior managers and those responsible for delivering the objectives of the activity been involved?
- How will success be measured? What indicators will be used to provide early indication that something is changing?

Are there any examples that might help me?

A risk breakdown structure (RBS) is a hierarchy diagram with an area or source of risk at the top, broken down into various risk areas (Figure 5.7).

Figure 5.7 Basic risk breakdown structure

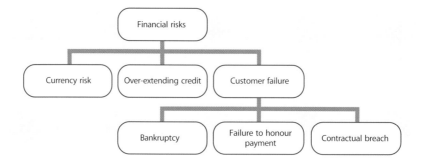

The RBS can be broken down into as many levels as is sensible. It is used to label or categorize risks (using labels such as PESTLE – see Chapter 4, section 'Strategic perspective', or people/process/tools or specialist product labels as defined by the organization). These structures will help later to identify appropriate owners to develop responses.

Enter data in a Risk Register (noting that you may want to use more than one RBS) (Table 5.1).

Table 5.1 Start of the Risk Register

ID	Category	Cause	Event	Effect
R001	Legal	Source of risk	Area of uncertainty	Impact on activity

Try creating a cause and effect diagram to assess risks or mitigation options. Once a risk has been identified, just keep on asking why this might occur, and work towards the left until you reach the root cause. This can easily be captured using a mind map (see Figure 5.8).

Figure 5.8 Root cause analysis diagram

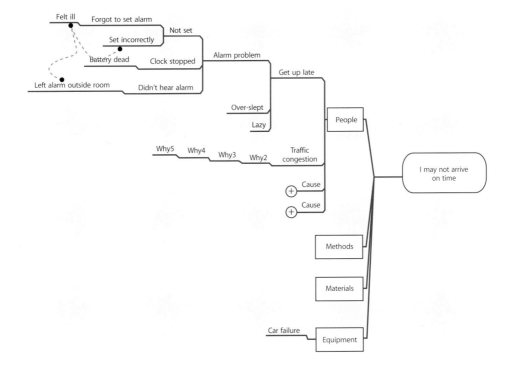

Managing Successful Programmes (MSP) (see 'Further information' at the end of this publication) provides a Risk Checklist in the form of a structured set of questions which can assist in the identification of risks in a programme under the following headings:

- Strategic Level:
  - Other programmes
  - Other initiatives within the organization
  - Inter-programme dependencies
  - Political pressures
- Programme Level:
  - Changing requirements and objectives
  - Programme Definition
  - Management skills
  - Inter-project dependencies
- Project Level:
  - Project risks
  - Third-party resources
- Operational Level:
  - Transfer of deliverables to operations
  - Acceptability within business operations
  - Acceptability to stakeholders.

ASSESS – ESTIMATE

The first task in the Assess step is to estimate the probability and impact of the risks (Estimate step).

What is the purpose?

The primary goal of the Estimate step (risk estimation) is to assess the threats and opportunities to the organization in terms of their probability and impact. The proximity of risk will also be of interest to gauge how quickly the risk is likely to materialize if no action were taken. This will require an understanding of:

- The probability of the threats and opportunities in terms of how likely they are to occur
- The impact of each threat and opportunity in terms of the activity objectives
- The proximity of these risks and opportunities with regard to when they might materialize.

The Assess-Estimate process is described graphically in Figure 5.9. The inputs to this process step correspond to the outputs of the Identify the Risks step along with cost estimates and any specific industry characteristics.

Figure 5.9 The Estimate process definition and information flows

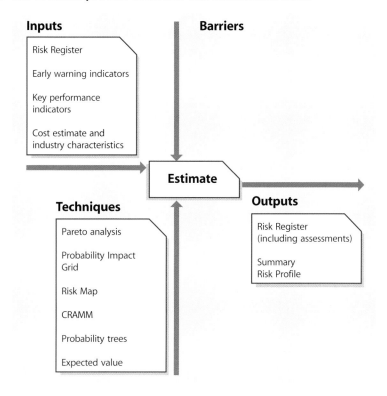

What are the benefits?

Good business relies on making informed decisions, which in turn requires good information. The benefits from the Estimate step are:

- Gaining an increased understanding of probability and impact to help identify the most important risks
- Knowing how quickly the risk is likely to materialize.

Do I have to do this?

Ranking or prioritizing helps to focus attention on the major risks requiring action. In order to be able to do that, knowledge about the likelihood and impact will need to be obtained and scores or measures will need to be assigned to them.

Producing a Summary Risk Profile will show whether the risks are acceptable or whether they need to be referred to a higher authority.

What happens if I don't do this?

Failing to do this step may mean failure to account for the risks altogether, or perhaps focusing on the wrong risks. The extent of the exposure when the risks materialize will not be understood.

How do I do this?

Subject-matter experts, project teams and relevant stakeholders are rich sources of information. By asking lots of questions and doing some research, the answers to questions such as these will become available:

- How likely is the risk?
- What kind of effect will it have?
- Where will the effects be felt?
- Who will it affect?
- How much will it cost if it happens?
- When might it happen?
- Will it affect the schedule?
- What will be the effect on quality?

Additional research may involve a review of:

- Stakeholder and organizational experience
- Lessons Learned reports
- Logs and registers from previous activities
- Historical data
- Industry figures.

Techniques that can be used to assist in this step include:

- Pareto analysis – to focus attention on risks which have the greatest impact
- Probability impact grid – to qualitatively rank the identified risks
- Risk map – to communicate the severity of the identified risks using a diagram
- Summary Risk Profile – a risk map including a risk tolerance line
- Probability trees – diagrams to assist the understanding of risk events resulting from various circumstances. A probability tree can be used to predict an outcome in a qualitative way when historical data is used to populate the likelihood of each circumstance happening
- Expected value – a weighted outcome of risk significance based on probability of impact and cost of impact
- CRAMM – a formal risk analysis and management method developed by the Central Computer and Telecommunications Agency (CCTA).

To focus attention on the major risks requiring action, ranking or prioritization is required. In order to be able to do that, gain knowledge about the likelihood and impact from the material collected above, and assign estimates or measures to them. Predefined scales for probability will assist in developing a common understanding of the way probability is expressed (Table 5.2).

Table 5.2 Probability scale

Probability	Code	Measure
Very low	VL	Very unlikely to occur: 0–5%
Low	L	Unlikely to occur: 6–20%
Medium	M	Fairly likely to occur: 21–50%
High	H	More likely to occur than not: 51–80%
Very high	VH	Very likely to occur: greater than 80%

Similarly, predefined scales can be used for describing impacts. When coming up with impact scales, take into account factors such as cost, time, safety and legal considerations. For example, Table 5.3 shows what a scale for impact might look like where time is not a critical factor to a schedulee.

Table 5.3 Impact scale

Impact	Code	Measure
Very low	VL	Less than 2 days' delay
Low	L	Small schedule slip: less than 2 weeks
Medium	M	Significant slip: between 2 weeks and 2 months
High	H	Large delay: between 2 and 3 months
Very high	VH	Major delay: more than 3 months

Scales can also be used to describe proximity rather than using simple date stamps (Table 5.4).

Table 5.4 Proximity scales

Project scale	Programme scale	Other scale
Imminent	Imminent	1 month
Within Stage	Within Tranche	3 months
Within Project	Within Programme	1 year
Outside Project	Outside Programme	More than 1 year

Having assessed probability and impact, this data should be recorded in the Risk Register (Table 5.5).

Table 5.5 Updated Risk Register

ID	Category	Cause	Event	Effect	Probability	Impact	Proximity
R001	Legal	Source of risk	Area of uncertainty	Impact on activity	Medium	High	Imminent

How do I get to the next step in the process?

The outputs needed to proceed to the next step are:

- Risk Register – a record of all identified risks relating to an initiative or activity, updated to include probability and impact in order to understand those risks which have a major impact on the activity and those which have minor impact
- Summary Risk Profile – a graphical representation of the information found in the Risk Register.

What questions should I ask to get to the next step?

- Is there a good degree of confidence in the analysis performed, and if there is not, are there plans for further work to get better estimates?
- How informed are the estimates made for probability, impact and proximity (that is, are they wild guesses, ballpark figures, based on assumptions or rigorously derived)?
- Have all assumptions been documented?

Are there any examples that might help me?

A qualitative assessment of risk called risk profiling may be done to see how important a particular risk event may be. In the example in Figure 5.10, a consultancy company is assessing the risk of a particular engagement.

Figure 5.10 Example risk assessment

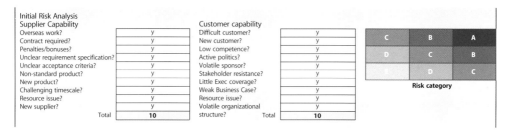

Depending on the output (A, B, C or D), a different action plan would be required. For example, see Table 5.6.

Table 5.6 Example responses

Category	Definition
A	Mitigation Strategy identified and approved for implementation Weekly status reporting to project board
B	Mitigation Strategy identified and approved for implementation Weekly monitoring of risk triggers
C	Mitigation Strategy identified Weekly monitoring of risk triggers
D	Risk triggers monitored
E	Ignore

EDF Energy has a number of impact matrices for each of Financial, Sustainability, Legal, Brand and Reputation, Governmental and Regulatory, Business Continuity, Safety, Customers and Employees. Table 5.7 is an example for the Safety impact scale (HSE is the Health & Safety Executive in the UK).

Table 5.7 EDF Energy 'Safety' impact scale

Impact	Code	Measure
Very low	VL	Minor injuries: accidental outcome
Low	L	Minor injuries: adverse outcome from HSE Major injuries: accidental outcome
Medium	M	Major injuries: adverse outcome from HSE Single fatality: accidental outcome
High	H	Single fatality: adverse outcome from HSE Potential criminal prosecution
Very high	VH	Multiple fatalities: adverse outcome from HSE Potential criminal prosecution

A Summary Risk Profile may be constructed from data recorded in the Risk Register. This can help to increase the visibility of risks (Figure 5.11).

Figure 5.11 Summary Risk Profile

Prob. / Impact	VL	L	M	H	VH
VH				① ③	
H	②				④
M		⑧		⑥	
L		⑩		⑦	
VL	⑨		②		⑤

Risk tolerance line

The Summary Risk Profile represents a situation at a specific point in time. It is effectively a snapshot of the risk environment at that time. The numbered markers in the matrix represent unique risk identifiers used in the Risk Register on which this is based. The dotted line is the risk tolerance line. The idea is that the risk above and to the right of this line represents risks that the organization will not tolerate except under special circumstances. For example, if the diagram represented the situation on a project, the Project Manager would refer risks 1, 3 and 4 to the Project Board.

ASSESS – EVALUATE

The second task in the Assess step is risk evaluation – to evaluate the overall effect of the risks on the activity being undertaken (Evaluate step).

What is the purpose?

The primary goal of the Evaluate step within the Assess process is to understand the net effect of the identified threats and opportunities on an activity when aggregated together. This may include preparing, for example, the following:

- An estimated monetary value (EMV) calculation, which records the weighted average of the anticipated impact
- A risk model, which aggregates the risks together using a simulation technique
- A net present value (NPV) calculation using an accepted discount rate.

The Assess-Evaluate process is described graphically in Figure 5.12. The inputs to this process step correspond to the outputs of the Assess-Estimate step.

Figure 5.12 The Evaluate process definition and information flows

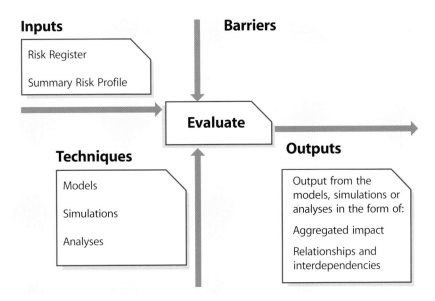

What are the benefits?

The benefit of performing this step is to see how the Strategic, Programme, Project and Operational business of the organization can be affected by risk overall. For example, a programme will not be able to deliver its stated benefit if each of the projects within the programme is delivered late. Be very careful here; there may be some 'outliers' which might need to be considered, such as a number of late projects possibly masking one critical project going badly wrong.

Use this step to make informed and well-reasoned assessments of the relationships between the risks. One person's view of risk may be quite different from another person's view. For example, in the 'Identify the Risks' step, a Project Manager may have scored a risk as 'high'. However, the Programme Manager may have a different scoring mechanism and see this risk as 'medium' or 'low', since this particular project may be 'small' compared with others in the programme. Aggregation needs to be done from the view of the person requiring the data.

Do I have to do this?

Yes, to understand the net effect of all the risks. Also, this step will help in describing the inter-relationship between specific threats and opportunities, and what the strength of the correlation may be.

What happens if I don't do this?

Without this analysis, there is a danger that decisions will be made without a real understanding of the data available, and not knowing which risks are going to pose the greatest threats or opportunities for the business.

How do I do this?

In order to conduct the Evaluate step, there are a number of techniques available to use depending on the level of detail and accuracy of information required:

- Models – a model representing the effect the risks may have on the business
- Simulation – used to obtain a probability distribution of the likely outcome of an activity
- Percentiles – used to provide confidence levels of the outcome of a simulation
- Monte Carlo simulation – a specific example of a simulation model
- Latin hypercube – a specific example of a simulation model
- Critical path analysis – the identification of activities that depend on one another to determine which activities are critical to the completion of a project
- Sensitivity analysis – a model to determine how a variable can affect a required outcome
- Cash flow analysis – to understand cash received and spent by a business during a defined period of time
- Portfolio analysis – to understand how the risks in each activity may affect the overall portfolio of programmes and projects
- Cost benefit analysis – a relationship of the costs of an activity to the monetary benefit assigned to the outcome derived from the activity
- Markov chain – used to model a change of state
- Utility theory – used to state the desirability of an outcome into a non-monetary measure.

How do I get to the next step in the process?

The outputs needed to proceed to the next step are:

- Aggregated Impact – showing the net effect of the threat and opportunity assessments when combined together
- Relationship and Interdependencies – showing the inter-relationship between specific threats and opportunities and what the strength of the correlation is.

What questions should I ask to get to the next step?

- What is the net effect of all these risks on the business?
- Are there any opportunities to capitalize on?
- Have the risks which will have most effect on the outcomes of the activity been understood?

- Have the organization's risks been spread across different areas of the business?
- Are all the risks in the same area?

Are there any examples that might help me?

- Strategic risks: in the 'Identify the Risks' step, a Risk Register was created with each risk tagged with a Risk Category to identify a specific risk area. To perform aggregation, simply filter those risks with a specific Risk Category. Alternatively, view risks through another category – for example, use customer-related categories such as market share or customer satisfaction. Do not restrict Risk Category to a single type.
- Programme risks: in the Business Case for each of the projects within the programme, think about the top three risks that could affect each of the project's outcomes, and present a sensitivity analysis for the whole programme against one of the outcomes. For example, a resourcing company wishes to attain a certain level of revenue from selling staff; depending on the cost rate of the staff, the number of days needed to be sold in order to break even could be charted. (The break-even point is defined as being the number of billable days in a month when the overheads are covered by the gross margin on associate/staff activity. It assumes that average sales price and overheads remain constant.) Figure 5.13 shows that if associate staff are bought at £400 per day, the break-even point will be achieved at day 30. If the rate is £600 per day, the break-even point is not reached until day 50.

Figure 5.13 Example sensitivity graph

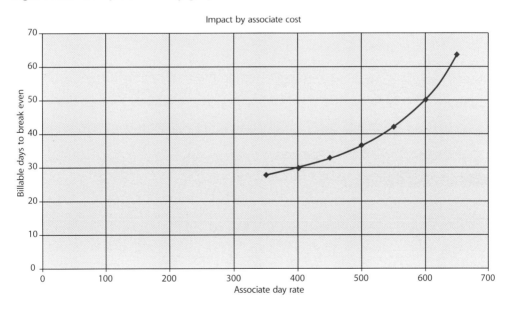

- Project risks: Define the risks that could affect the project's success and perform an EMV calculation
- Operational risks: Relate the risks to your operational dashboards by analysing the early warning indicators to see if the operational targets can be met.

PLAN

What is the purpose?

The primary goal of the Plan step is to prepare specific management responses to the threats and opportunities identified, ideally to remove or reduce the threats and to maximize the opportunities. Attention to this step ensures as far as possible that the business and its staff are not taken by surprise if a risk materializes.

The Plan process is described graphically in Figure 5.14. The inputs to this process step correspond to the outputs of the Assess-Evaluate step with additional external input.

Figure 5.14 Plan process definition and information flows

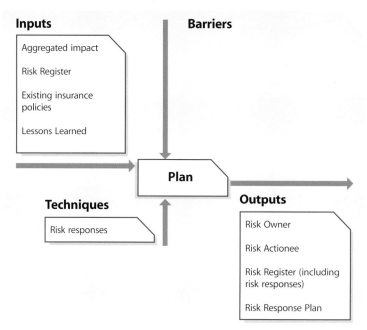

What are the benefits?

Planning provides the baseline against which progress can be monitored.

The Plan step can help to decide whether or not to invest in an activity – if the activity is too risky, or there are other activities with very similar risks, then do not do this activity as well.

Do I have to do this?

A planned response to a threat to minimize its impact on the business is essential. Also consider how to exploit the opportunities that have been identified. Once a response has been determined, allocate a 'Risk Actionee', who is responsible for ensuring that the actions are completed.

To gain commitment from contributors and recipients, define the communications of what needs to be done, how, when and by whom in the Risk Response Plan.

What happens if I don't do this?

A frequent excuse for rushing or sidestepping is: 'the project had such tight deadlines that we didn't have time to plan'. It can be demonstrated time and again that every day spent planning will save or gain as many days later on.

How do I do this?

In the Evaluate step, the risks which would affect the outcomes of the activity should have been identified. In the Plan step this is followed up by:

- Identifying a possible risk response
- Re-assessing the probability, impact and expected value, assuming that the risk response identified will be implemented
- Deciding whether or not to implement the plan
- Assigning a Risk Actionee to implement the proposed action.

A number of techniques are available to help with planning, aimed at risk efficiency. The categorizations of Reduction, Removal, Transfer, Retention, Share, Realization, Enhancement and Exploitation are explained in the following tables. Responses to threats are shown in Table 5.8.

Table 5.8 Threat responses

Reduction	Proactive actions taken to reduce the probability or impact
Removal	(For example) change of scope to remove risk
Transfer	Move responsibility to a third party
Retention	A conscious and deliberate decision not to execute a risk response action
Share	Offset some pain and gain using a partner

A special form of Reduction should also be considered using Controls. Both probability and impact can be reduced by Controls. There are four Control options (Table 5.9).

Table 5.9 Control options

Directive	Ensure a particular outcome is achieved
Preventive	Limit undesirable outcome
Detective	Capture of information for use in the future
Corrective	Correct undesirable outcomes that have been realized

Various categories of Transfer need to be considered (Table 5.10).

Table 5.10 Transfer categories

Insurance	Insure using a third party against financial loss
Self-insurance	Insure using own organization against financial loss
Insurance captive	Participate in the insurance portfolio of the parent organization
Contractual transfer	Financial consequences transferred to a third party

Exploit any opportunities that have been identified by choosing suitable responses (Table 5.11).

Table 5.11 Opportunity responses

Realization	Identifying and seizing an opportunity
Enhancement	Seizing and improving on an identified opportunity
Exploitation	Identifying and seizing multiple benefits

Tables 5.8–5.11 are explained more fully in the M_o_R Guidance.

How do I get to the next step in the process?

The outputs needed to proceed to the next step are:

- Risk Owner – identifies the Risk Owner
- Risk Actionee – identifies the Risk Actionee
- Risk Register – updated Risk Register with risk responses and residual impact estimates
- Risk Response Plan – optional document to record details of all risk response actions and to help with the monitoring and control of these actions.

What questions should I ask to get to the next step?

What is the risk appetite (or pain thresholds)? For example, what are the effects on a company with a turnover of £10 million if the company makes a loss? Losses of less than £100,000 may not have much effect, but losses of £1 million may mean the company collapses. If a strategic risk could cause the company to be hurt (i.e. to go beyond the pain threshold), then have a risk response action plan!

Plan for the inevitable: if you are in the power distribution business, then you know that occasionally the weather will have an adverse effect; planning to cope with storm damage ahead of time would be a prudent thing to do.

Are there any examples that might help me?

Consider the following. A company decides to demonstrate a new prototype around the world, and plans to visit 15 capital cities in three months, travelling mainly by air. The company's future success depends on gaining orders from these demonstrations; losses to the business have been estimated to be £500,000. The replacement cost of a new prototype is £50,000. Should the company:

- Build a spare costing another £50,000

  or

- Insure the prototype against loss at a cost of £4,000

  or

- Just accept that the prototype may be lost, costing the company £500,000 + £50,000.

Normally, only one response action would be planned. However, here the company should take all three mitigating actions:

- It is common practice to build spares
- It is common practice to insure
- But ultimately the organization takes the risk when it all goes wrong; try to reduce both the probability and impact!

IMPLEMENT

What is the purpose?

The primary goal of the Implement step is to ensure that the planned risk management actions are implemented and monitored as to their effectiveness, and corrective action is taken when responses do not match expectations.

The Implement process is described graphically in Figure 5.15. The inputs to this process step correspond to the outputs of the Assess-Evaluate step.

Figure 5.15 The Implement process definition and information flows

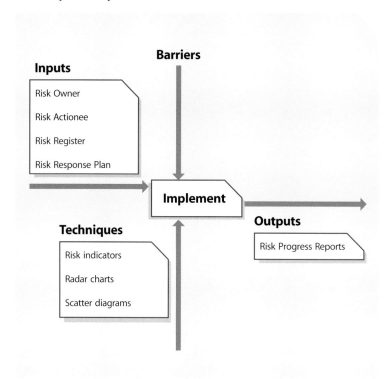

What are the benefits?

The activities here are designed to ensure that the planned responses have actually been implemented, that their effectiveness is monitored and that action is taken to address risk actions which have not been effective. The main benefit is to see what effect the plans are having on the status of the risks that are being monitored. Also, if any new risks materialize, have a plan for dealing with them.

Do I have to do this?

If this step is not done then all the previous work will have been in vain. There is no point in having good plans and then not executing them. In addition, consider what to do when a previously unidentified risk materializes that requires immediate management attention.

What happens if I don't do this?

If there is no implementation, then there will be no information available on the progress towards mitigating threats or maximizing opportunities.

How do I do this?

This is not the end of the process and should not be thought of as the last step. Once risks have been identified, assessed and planned, it is essential that the plans are executed, monitored and controlled to see what effect they are having on the risk. Moreover, as new risks are identified, the process should begin again.

The Implement step can be executed in a number of ways:

- Ensure that Risk Progress Reports are produced showing what actions have been completed and whether the actions are having the desired effect
- Conduct Risk Response Action audits to measure the effectiveness of the Risk Response Plan
- Hold regular risk reviews to monitor progress and make changes to the Risk Response Plan
- Use Earned Value Analysis to inspect deviations from the plan; check to see whether these deviations are due to the occurrence of risks which had already been identified
- Maintain Performance Dashboards to show how the actions are achieving the desired results.

There are a few techniques available to help:

- Risk indicators – to show the level of acceptability of a risk
- Radar chart – visually displays risk attributes on a number of axes
- Scatter diagram – provides a visual display of event concentration.

How do I get to the next step in the process?

The outputs needed to proceed to the next step are:

- Risk Progress Reports – to provide regular progress information to management on risk management within a particular activity.

What questions should I ask to get to the next step?

- Are the plans having any effect?
- Are the numbers of risks being reduced?
- Are the actions being completed?

Are there any examples that might help me?

The OGC Rapid Risk Check tool is a profiling tool which groups risk into six categories. The results of the assessments can be used to show how risks have changed over the period (see Figure 5.16). This is one of the diagrams that could be included in the Risk Progress Report. The risks are divided into:

- **Inherent risks** – risks that relate to the organization itself:
  - Business vision
  - Business process
  - Business environment and constraints
- **Acquired risks** – risks that arise as a consequence of doing the project:
  - Scope of programme, project or procurement
  - Project organization and control
  - Team capability, experience and support.

A major benefit of this tool is that it can be used to perform comparisons of risks over time, or used to compare two different scenarios.

Figure 5.16 Comparison of Risk Profiles at two assessment points

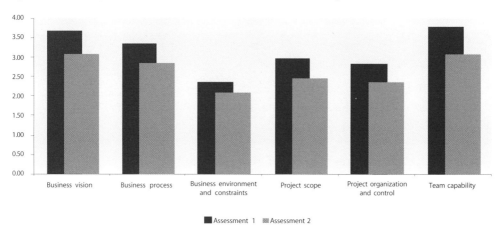

The scale on the y-axis is the risk assessment score from the model which can have a value from 1 to 5.

The Risk Progress Report could include simple charts showing the risk status from the Risk Register (Figure 5.17).

Figure 5.17 Risk Progress Report diagram

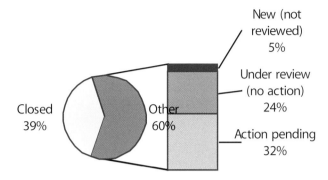

COMMUNICATING RISK

What is the purpose?

It is important for management to engage with staff across the organization to ensure that:

- Everyone understands the organization's risk appetite
- Everyone understands the benefits of effective risk management
- Each level of management actively seeks and receives appropriate and regular assurance about the management of risk within their control
- The procurement team understands the requirement for making risk ownership explicit within contracts and service level agreements
- Transferable Lessons Learned are communicated
- There is no misunderstanding over the respective risk priorities within and across each business perspective
- Any organization providing outsourcing services has adequate risk management skills and processes.

What does this mean?

Many things need to be communicated during the execution of the risk process – here are a few examples:

- Describe the business objectives and how they are linked to operational risks and actions
- List the key risks to be monitored
- Ensure that everyone understands their responsibility for assignment and communication of key business risks
- Report on risk action planning
- Report on how a crisis will be managed
- Present the risk processes diagrammatically, noting key control points.

Are there any examples that might help me?

Firstly, establish clear responsibilities for achieving risk communication objectives, and identify who needs to do what, to ensure that the objectives are met. Secondly, put in place a Communications Plan.

Once a Stakeholder Map (see Appendix A) has been completed, communication planning can begin. This is carried out to ensure that all stakeholder groups and people who need to be influenced most are addressed. The Communications Plan begins by thinking about whom to communicate with, about what, how and when. Enter this data in a simple table (Table 5.12).

Table 5.12 Communications planning

Audience	Purpose and objectives	Type of message	Communication channel	When, where, by whom
Programme Managers	Communicate revised Risk Management Policy	General: reasons for change with content	Presentation and workshop	Date; location; Risk Director

- Identify audience – ensure that different audiences receive the necessary communications, and group each audience to the level and type of communications they require
- Identify the purpose and objectives of the communications for each group – the objective may be to build general awareness, solicit buy-in, increase participation, etc.
- Identify the types of message to communicate – for example:
  - General background – ask questions such as what is it for; how does it fit the strategy?
  - Benefits of M_o_R – such as what are the benefits, why M_o_R and how will it benefit the business?
  - Cultural change – for example, how is it aligned to current values; what do we stop doing?
  - Personal concerns – such as what is in it for me and how does it affect the organization?
- Identify the best communication channel for the intended communication
  - Plan the communication – who will prepare it, who will do it, how it will be communicated etc.

Be sensitive to all of the people you are trying to communicate with; the Inter-Departmental Liaison group on Risk Assessment (ILGRA) suggests a framework for communications called the 'ECCB formula' (Table 5.13).

Table 5.13 The ILGRA ECCB formula

Empathy	Engage your audience; do not switch them off. Think through what you have in common with them, and what might make them warm to you, or reject you as having nothing to say to them. If you are in a debate and the audience engages emotionally with your opponent but not with you, you will lose irrespective of the merits of your argument
Concern	Always show respect for people and their concerns, no matter how illogical they may seem to you. If you do not show that you care about their concerns, people will never trust you
Commitment	Provide evidence that you do not just say you have people's interests at heart, but that your track record, or your approach, is proven to do so. Why should people believe that you will be successful in dealing with this risk? Think through who might erode or reinforce your credibility and how to involve or deal with them.
Benefit	It is vital to articulate the pros and cons of the approach decided upon in terms with which the audience can identify. Be open about dis-benefits of your solution, as well as benefits. If you are giving people information on which to base their own decisions, explain how the pros and cons are likely to vary with individuals' circumstances.

Occasionally, an organization will need to go public with its risk management approach. International Power, in its *Summary Annual Report 2006* to shareholders, states the company's approach to risk management:

'There is a continuous process for identifying, evaluating and managing the key risks faced by the Group. Activities are coordinated by the Risk Committee which is chaired by the Chief Financial Officer (CFO) and comprises Executive Directors, and other regional directors and senior managers.'

The principal risks and exposures are listed as:

- Financial Risks
- Market and trading risks
- Fuel supply risks
- Country and political risks
- Construction and operational risks
- Health, safety and environmental (HS&E) risks.

Do I have to do this?

Stakeholders have a vital role in implementing changes to the management of risk in any organization, especially when adopting new ways of working. Without their support, the risk management activities will not be successful. This support will only be gained by relevant and timely communication of the issues that are most relevant to each stakeholder. This is achieved by a structured approach to identification, profiling and communicating to stakeholders.

What happens if I do not do this?

Without a systematic approach, it is likely that there will be two key failings:

- Wrong messages are communicated to the stakeholders
- Stakeholders are not properly identified. Individuals are labelled as stakeholders of the programme when they are not; and others are not identified, and therefore not communicated with.

What are the benefits?

Stakeholders become an effective, positive and supportive additional resource on the programme and related projects, rather than being a liability.

Product outlines

A

Appendix A: Product outlines

M_o_R Guidance lists a number of product outlines:

- *Issue Log*
- *Risk Improvement Plan*
- *Risk Management Strategy*
- *Risk Management Policy*
- Risk Management Process Guide
- Risk Progress Report
- *Risk Register*
- Risk Response Plan
- Stakeholder Map.

To capture and communicate the key practices of risk management, it is common to create a management of risk approach composed of a number of living documents; these are italicized in the list above, and are described fully in the M_o_R Guidance and other related publications.

The Product Outlines described in this appendix will help most when thinking about embarking on risk management implementation.

RISK IMPROVEMENT PLAN

Purpose

To provide a record of the current status of management of risk cultural awareness within the organization, the behavioural targets that are to be achieved and an appropriate time period in which to achieve them, and the mechanisms/methods planned to be used to achieve the cultural change (these need to be appropriate to the culture and ethos of the organization).

Background

It is important to ensure that the tone of, and the cultural approach to, the risk awareness programme fit in with the ethos of the company. Once an approach has been agreed, a Risk Improvement Plan should be developed (with key dates and targets) and implemented.

Composition

Typically a Risk Improvement Plan (see Table A.1) will include as a minimum:

- Current date – the date the cultural plan is agreed, or the date the existing behaviour is assessed and recorded
- Category group – the group of individuals being targeted for this particular improvement initiative – for example, executives, senior managers, technical staff or secretaries
- Existing behaviours – a description detailing the assessment of current behaviour towards the different aspects of management of risk
- Target behaviour – a description detailing the preferred/target behaviour towards the different aspects of management of risk
- Target date – the time by which you wish to target the change in behaviour
- Mechanisms – the mechanisms that will be used to change the behaviour towards, or understanding of, management of risk
- Measurement – how the change in behaviour will be measured.

Current date

This is the date the report was prepared.

Category group

From the Stakeholder Map, identify the stakeholder groups that are targeted for improvement; especially consider those showing dark and semi-dark shading in the stakeholder matrix (see Figure A.2 later in this appendix).

Existing behaviour

From the stakeholder analysis, identify the behaviours that need to be changed. Identify specific instances that stand out – for example:

- There was no mention of the initiative in a recent briefing
- A particular person was always being negative
- You never get chance to talk to the sponsor.

Target behaviour

Think about the future – what are people saying about the activity? Try to capture specific items that would be nice to achieve, for example:

- The initiative was mentioned in the management report
- The sponsor always talks about the activity every time they meet me.

Target date

Set a realistic timescale for this change of behaviour to happen; it will not occur overnight!

Mechanisms

- What action is required to make this happen?
- What sort of communications need to take place?
- Is there a 'vision' or 'elevator pitch' that each member of the team can talk about in two minutes?

Measurement

What measures are in place that will indicate achievement of the desired behaviour? The measure needs to be SMART (Specific, Measurable, Achievable, Relevant and Time-framed).

Table A.1 Example Risk Improvement Plan

Category group	Existing behaviour	Target behaviour	Target date	Mechanisms	Measurement
Management Team	Activity never gets mentioned in monthly management reports	Activity gets mentioned in monthly management reports	Within three months	Talk to sponsor. Provide input each month. Follow up with editor	Activity mentioned at least every other month

RISK RESPONSE PLAN

Purpose

To record details of all risk response actions and to help with the monitoring, control and reporting of these actions. This is an optional document as it may be decided to hold this information with the Risk Register against each risk.

Background

Risk responses are contained within a Risk Register or recorded individually with each response on a separate page of a document.

Composition

Typically a response plan (see Table A.2) will include as a minimum:

- Risk identification (ID)
- Risk description
- Impact in terms of cost and time
- Risk response category
- Actions to respond to the threat or opportunity (it is common for there to be multiple actions)
- Risk Owner
- Risk Actionee

- Date by which the actions are to be implemented
- Anticipated cost of the response
- Any secondary threats or opportunities that may arise from the response.

Risk ID

A unique identifier linking the risk to an activity.

Risk description

A well-articulated expression of the cause-risk effect.

Impact in terms of cost and time

Based on known figures or estimates, or based on published severity scales.

Response category

This will be selected from the options described in the Risk Management Strategy.

Actions to respond to the threat or opportunity

Record of chosen responses together with trigger dates.

Risk Owner

Named individual responsible for management and control of risks.

Risk Actionee

Named individual who takes direction from and supports the Risk Owner; they are assigned to the implementation of risk response actions.

Date

When the actions are to be implemented.

Anticipated costs

An estimate of costs and resource usage/effort to help balance the response against the consequences of the risk, and to assist with scheduling.

Secondary threats

As a result of implementing this response plan, further risks may be introduced.

Opportunities

As a result of implementing this response plan, potential opportunities may present themselves.

Table A.2 Example Risk Response Plan

Risk Response Plan	
Risk ID	1.2
Risk description	Due to potential supplier financial issues, there is a risk that they may produce items which do not meet our quality criteria, which means that rework will be required and may delay our schedule
Impact: Cost	£20,000
Impact: Time	Five weeks
Risk response category	Reduction
Response actions	1. Preventive: provide financial assistance to supplier; embed our own quality personnel with supplier to act as mentors and to act as early warning sensors
	2. Preventive: assess, select and engage with alternative supplier
Risk Owner	Chief Engineer
Risk Actionee	1. Financial Director, Quality Consultant
	2. Procurement Manager, Chief Engineer
Implementation date	Next milestone date less five weeks
Estimated cost	Financial Director rate x 4 days Quality Consultant rate x 40 days + on-site expenses Procurement Manager rate x 30 days Chief Engineer rate x 10 days
Secondary threats	Actions divert staff from other activities
Opportunities	Gets current supplier back to stability Gain another supplier, providing fallback position in the future

RISK PROGRESS REPORT

Purpose

To provide regular progress information to management on risk management within a particular activity.

Background

The purpose of this report is to provide progress information to management. It describes risk management within a particular activity. The report should be produced regularly at the frequency indicated in the related Communications Plan. It is an output of the Implement step of the management of risk process.

The report is important because it gives insight to the effectiveness of the risk mitigation actions selected. It can instil confidence in the level to which risk exposure is being controlled.

Composition

Typically a progress report (see Table A.3) will include as a minimum:

- Progress of planned M_o_R actions
- Effectiveness of implemented actions
- Trend analysis of closed and new risks
- Insurance requirements
- Spend against contingencies
- Numbers of risks emerging in the different risk categories
- Movement of risk against the key performance indicators
- Anticipated emerging risks that will require specific management attention.

This information may be incorporated within other progress reports if appropriate.

Progress of planned M_o_R actions

Are the risk management actions being implemented as planned, and are the planned outcomes and measures visible?

Effectiveness of implemented actions

Are the actions having the desired effect on reducing the potential impact and/or reducing the probability of the risks? Were appropriate actions identified and selected?

Trend analysis of closed and new risks

Are risks being closed as they expire (the time has now passed when that risk might have affected the objective)? Or have the actions dealt with the situation, and are new risks being identified, recorded and managed?

Insurance requirements

Is there sufficient cover for the current and outstanding risks? Are premiums still in force for closed risks?

Spend against contingencies

For tolerated or accepted risks, have the planned amounts being spent (cost/time/resource) minimized the consequences as forecasted?

Numbers of risks emerging in the different risk categories

Are new risks emerging? Why?

Movement of risk against the key performance indicators

Are the performance targets getting closer to the planned values?

Anticipated emerging risks that will require specific management attention

Are any of the new risks deemed to be unacceptable – that is, are they above the defined level of tolerance?

Table A.3 Example Risk Response Plan

Risk Progress Report	
Planned actions against Risk ID	1.2
Action 1 progress	Provide financial assistance to supplier: Financial Director has reviewed supplier's financial position and has agreed to an early payment schedule in return for discounts. Contracts to be finalized
	Embed our own quality personnel with supplier to act as mentors and to act as early warning sensors: our staff have identified cause of quality issues and recommended corrective actions with target completion dates
Action 2 progress	Assess, select and engage with alternative supplier: Chief Engineer has identified and visited three potential suppliers and has recommended selection based on reference customers. Next step is for contracts to be signed and the new supplier's details to be entered into our procurement and quality systems. Completion expected in March – on target
Effectiveness of actions	1. Cost has been equivalent to cost of impact, but will now maintain schedule
	2. Will probably not require new supplier, but selection process was efficient and we do now have a fallback position
Trend analysis	Will not close risks until contracts have been signed and next milestone has been passed
Spend against contingencies	Financial Director rate x 2 days (4 planned)
	Quality Consultant rate x 40 days + on-site expenses (as per plan)
	Procurement Manager rate x 3 days (30 planned)
	Chief Engineer rate x 9 days (10 planned)
New risks emerging	Currently reorganizing Quality Team's work as a result of temporarily losing Quality Consultant
	Quality Consultant has indicated that they wish to work full-time with supplier. This may necessitate an additional recruitment activity

STAKEHOLDER MAP

Purpose

To document stakeholders – that is, all parties (individuals or groups) that have an interest in the outcome of the proposed activity. This may include individuals or groups outside the organization. The interests of each stakeholder are identified and the map is used to ensure all interests are catered for, which includes keeping them informed and accepting feedback.

Background

The Stakeholder Map is an output from the culmination of work undertaken on stakeholder analysis. A stakeholder is anyone affected by a decision and interested in its outcome. This can include individuals or groups, both inside and outside the organization. The stakeholder analysis is a piece of work undertaken to assess the influence and importance of each individual stakeholder or stakeholder group. The Stakeholder Map is typically shown as a matrix, detailing individual stakeholders or groups of stakeholders and their particular interests, along with the communication route and frequency for each stakeholder or group of stakeholders.

Composition

Typically a Stakeholder Map will include as a minimum:

- List of stakeholders
- List of interests (i.e. issues that concern each individual stakeholder or members of a stakeholder group, their attitude towards aspects of the situation that present a risk, and the extent to which they can influence the way that the risk is to be addressed)
- Matrix of stakeholders to interest and the relative importance of the project/magnitude of the risks to each.

List of stakeholders

Identify the stakeholder groups/individual stakeholders using a simple table (Table A.4).

Table A.4 Stakeholder roles

Stakeholder groups/individuals	Roles
Group 1	P
Group 2	R, A
Group 3	C
etc.	

Roles can be one or more of the following: **P**roducer of something, **C**ontributor to the production of something, **R**eviewer or **A**cceptor of the deliverable.

Alternatively, the M_o_R Guidance promotes the use of RACI and RACI-VS diagrams to support stakeholder analysis (Figure A.1). The participating stakeholder roles reflected in these diagrams are: **R**esponsible, **A**ccountable, **C**onsulted, **I**nformed, **V**erifies and **S**igns-off.

Figure A.1 A simplified example of a RACI diagram

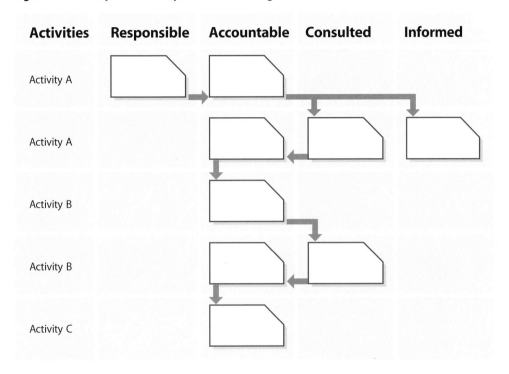

List of interests

For each member of a stakeholder group and each individual stakeholder, complete a simple stakeholder analysis (Table A.5).

Table A.5 Simple stakeholder analysis

Stakeholder group	Priority	Name	Attitude	Issues of concern or interests
Group 1		Name 1		
		Name 2		
		Name 3		
Group 2		Name 1		
		Name 2		
Group 3		Name 1		

Fill in the columns shown in Table A.5 as follows:

■ Priority – how important is this person to success? What influence do they have? A three-point scale with high, medium and low priorities may be used here.

■ Attitude – are the people supportive of your objectives? A five-point scale (e.g. very negative - -, negative -, neutral, positive +, very positive ++) may be used here.

■ Issues of concern – note any specific instances to justify the attitude, and any specific issues of concern or interests they may have.

Stakeholder matrix

Complete the picture showing the priorities and attitudes of the stakeholders. Actions should be taken with those stakeholders who have a medium and/or high influence and those who are negative and/or very negative towards your endeavour. In Figure A.2 the increasing density of the coloured areas indicates increasing importance of taking appropriate action. Such actions could be resolving conflicting objectives, representing end-user interests and reinforcing relationships.

Figure A.2 Stakeholder matrix template

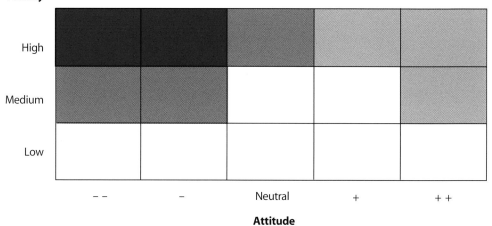

Activities

The charts produced here as part of the Stakeholder Map should be completed at the start of an activity and reviewed periodically, say every six months, or prior to a review of the Communications Plan.

Relationship

The Stakeholder Map should be used as an input to the communicate process and the Risk Improvement Plan.

Performing a healthcheck

B

Appendix B: Performing a healthcheck

Good risk management practice happens when the M_o_R principles are well applied. The management of risk healthcheck is a tool for checking the health of current risk management and for identifying areas where its application might be improved. It may be used for self-assessment, peer review or external assessment.

The healthcheck is most useful when preparing and carrying out an enterprise-wide assessment. It is also applicable for assessments of specific programmes, projects or operational activities. This healthcheck is only a starting point. It should be adapted to the particular assessment and nature of the business. The focus of the healthcheck is on the current practice of the management of risk and is evidence-based.

The healthcheck can be very useful when considering:

- New investments
- Business planning
- Preparing to implement M_o_R
- Improving the current state of risk management
- OGC Gateway™ Reviews
- Developing annual plans.

PROCESS

To be effective, the healthcheck should be formally administered and repeated to monitor changes over time. Each administration of the healthcheck will occur using the following steps:

Preparation > Data Collection > Data Analysis > Review and Report.

FRAMEWORK

The healthcheck assesses risk management practice. It is recommended that the 12 M_o_R principles are used as a framework for structuring the assessment.

Against each principle, review the questions provided by the M_o_R Guidance and consider whether they are appropriate for the organization (Table B.1). Develop further questions relevant to the organization and activity being assessed.

For each of the questions posed, what evidence is available to support the answers? Positive responses indicate that the principle is being applied correctly. Negative responses indicate that there may be a need to carry out some improvements in how a principle is being applied.

To answer the questions objectively and remove bias, it may be appropriate to engage a third party who has not been involved. This could be a suitably qualified member of another team, an internal or external auditor or an independent consultant.

If deficiencies are found with the implementation of any of the foundation principles, these should be addressed first, with recommendations for their improvement made in the report. Once foundation principles are in place, the secondary principles can be addressed.

Table B.1 Considerations for the 12 M_o_R principles

Principle	Consideration
Organizational context	The management of risk should reflect the context of the organization and the nature of the organizational activity under examination
Stakeholder involvement	The management of risk should involve all major stakeholders
Organizational objectives	The management of risk should be undertaken against clear objectives
M_o_R approach	An organization should develop an approach to the management of risk that reflects its objectives
Reporting	The governing body of an organization should receive, review and act on risk management reports
Roles and responsibilities	An organization should establish clear roles and responsibilities for the management of risk in terms of leadership, direction, controls, ongoing risk management, reporting and reviewing
Support structure	A structure to support the management of risk for the organizational activity under consideration should be established
Early warning indicators	An organization should establish early warning indicators for critical business activities as part of proactive risk management to provide information on the potential sources of risk
Review cycle	An organization should regularly review the risks the organization is facing and the policies, processes and plans it is adopting to manage them
Overcoming barriers to M_o_R	Management of risk should recognize and respond to the barriers to implementation
Supportive culture	An organization should establish the right culture for supporting risk management throughout the organization
Continual improvement	An organization should develop strategies to improve its risk management maturity to support best practice

Using maturity models

C

Appendix C: Using maturity models

MATURITY MODELS

Maturity models are a valuable tool in enabling organizations to benchmark their current risk management capability and maturity, and in understanding how and where improvement may be achieved. Maturity models are intended to provide a well-structured and detailed guide to facilitate the progressive incremental improvement in risk management practices.

With the aid of a maturity model, an organization can set realistic long-term goals for risk management, by having a clear understanding of its current maturity in terms of current working practices and the areas that require improvement.

PROCESS IMPROVEMENT

Learning organizations look to improve their processes to enhance their overall performance in an ever-changing and increasingly competitive environment. The benefits of risk management derived by organizations will depend directly on the level of maturity of their risk management practices.

Organizations are increasingly turning to maturity models for assessing and improving processes on the premise that the quality of a system or product is highly influenced by the quality of the process used to develop and maintain it.

Maturity models provide a direct way to describe, communicate and implement risk management process improvement. They describe an evolutionary improvement path from using ad hoc, immature processes to highly disciplined, effective, mature processes.

DEFINITION

The risk management maturity model is a reference model for appraising an organization's risk management competency and/or capability.

The maturity model provides:

- A starting point from which the organization can move forward
- A way of capturing the organization's previous experience and current capabilities
- A common language and terminology
- A communication tool to describe the current status and what is possible
- A framework for prioritizing actions

- A way of describing what improvement means
- A shared goal.

The maturity model levels are described in a matrix of levels and assessment criteria. The higher the level of risk maturity attained by an organization, the greater its prospects for successfully managing risk, and the lower its potential for failure.

Five levels are defined in the M_o_R Guidance. Each level is described in terms of the criteria that need to be met to demonstrate capability at that level. Although there is no limit to the number of criteria that can be used, most models contain fewer than 10, as above this number, assessments begin to get unwieldy. The five levels are:

- Initial – unaware or naïve of the need for risk management, or at a minimum is used on an ad-hoc basis
- Repeatable – trialling risk management techniques
- Defined – formal policies exist
- Managed – led by senior management, a robust framework is in place
- Optimizing – fully risk- and opportunity-aware culture, with performance gains made through informed decision-making.

The levels provide:

- Stepping stones for incremental improvement
- A realistic route to move from an immature, novice, naïve or initial state to a mature and capable state
- A tool for the objective judgement of the quality of risk management processes.

Figure C.1 shows diagrammatically the summary descriptions of each of the levels of maturity; a full definition is provided in the M_o_R Guidance.

Figure C.1 Risk management maturity model – description of the levels

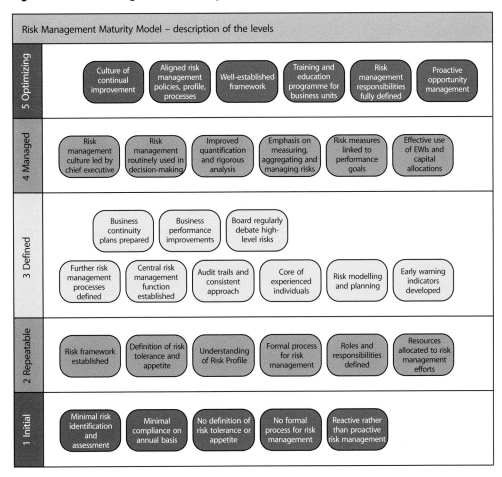

PROGRESSING BETWEEN MATURITY LEVELS

Once risk maturity within an organization has been assessed and a model has been constructed, steps can be undertaken to develop specific action plans for improving processes to attain the next level in the model. It is recognized that there are constraints in moving from one level to the next. Although these constraints are not insurmountable, they take management time and effort to overcome. For instance, to move from level 1 to level 2 it is common for organizations to address the following:

■ Developing a risk management process that is tailored to the organization
■ Defining the organization's risk appetite
■ Understanding, capturing and disseminating the anticipated sources of risk
■ Developing a risk terminology that will aid embedding risk management in the organization

- Promulgating the benefits of risk management using examples of completed risk management studies
- Developing straightforward risk management reporting
- Making risk management roles and responsibilities explicit.

BENEFITS OF USING A MATURITY MODEL

The growing popularity of maturity models and the breadth of their application stems from the benefits that they can offer organizations. The list below describes some of the primary benefits of maturity models.

- They provide organizations with a road map for process improvement that can be readily constructed, assimilated and communicated.
- They provide a vehicle for benchmarking risk management processes.
- They enable organizations to identify what needs to be done in order to improve current processes and increase their ability to manage threats and opportunities.
- They enable organizations to build an action plan of the activities they wish to embark on to improve their processes.
- They afford organizations the opportunity to assess the financial benefits obtained from one level of the model prior to committing resources to implementing the next level.
- When processes are understood and operating at their best, staff are motivated, morale and productivity are high, and the quality of outputs is also high. Even the finest people cannot perform at their best when working with immature processes.
- They enable the benefits of risk management to be realized in terms of minimizing costly project overruns, making informed decisions when selecting between options and making the risk ownership profile of different contracts transparent.
- They support organizations to reach their strategic objectives while at the same time conserving organizational resources.

Further
information

Further information

Do you think you are ready to learn more about M_o_R? The links and publications listed below will give you a greater level of understanding and put you in contact with the rest of the M_o_R community.

PUBLICATIONS

Your first stop will be the M_o_R manual. This is available in a variety of formats and can be purchased from the Best Management Practice website (www.best-management-practice.com):

Management of Risk: Guidance for Practitioners
ISBN 9780113310388

M_o_R Pocketbook
ISBN 9780113310661

Whilst there is an exhaustive list of references in the M_o_R manual, here are a few simple places to start to get more background to risk management.

General

Risk Management Standards (2002)
AIRMIC (The Association of Insurance and Risk Managers), ALARM (The National Forum for Risk Management in the Public Sector), IRM (The Institute of Risk Managers)
www.theirm.org/publications/PUstandard.html

HM Treasury/OGC(Office of Government Commerce)/NAO (National Audit Office)
Guidance on Early Management of the Risks to Successful Delivery
www.ogc.gov.uk/resource_toolkit.asp

HM Treasury (2004)
The Orange Book
Management of Risk – Principles and Concepts
www.hm-treasury.gov.uk

The Business Continuity Institute (w)
A Management Guide to Implementing Global Good Practice in Business Continuity Management
www.thebci.org/gpgdownloadpage.htm

Mercer Oliver Wyman (2005–2007)
What's Your Risk Appetite?
www.oliverwyman.com/ow/

UK Resilience
Communicating Risk
www.ukresilience.info/preparedness/risk.aspx

Strategic risk

A Director's Guide to Risk Management
Institute of Directors
ISBN 1904520448

Committee of Sponsoring Organizations of the Treadway Commission (COSO) (2004)
Enterprise Risk Management – Integrated Framework
Committee of Sponsoring Organizations of the Treadway Commission
www.coso.org/publications.htm

Programme risk

Office of Government Commerce (OGC) (2007)
Managing Successful Programmes
TSO (The Stationery Office)
ISBN 9780113310401

Max Wideman, R. (editor) (1992)
Project and Program Risk Management: A Guide to Managing Project Risks and Opportunities (PMBOK – Project Management Body Of Knowledge Handbooks)
Program Management Institute
ISBN 1880410060

Project risk

Office of Government Commerce (OGC) (2005)
Managing Successful Projects with PRINCE2, 4th edition
TSO (The Stationery Office)
ISBN 9780113309467

Project Risk Management SIG
Project Risk Analysis and Management Guide
APM (Association for Project Management)
ISBN 1903494125

Operational risk

Risk Communication: A Guide to Regulatory Practice
HSE (Health & Safety Executive)
www.hse.gov.uk

HM Treasury
Risk Management Assessment Model
www.hm-treasury.gov.uk

USEFUL LINKS

www.best-management-practice.com

www.usergroup.org.uk (the official Best Practice User Group for M_o_R)

www.efqm.org

ACCREDITATION

A form of self-help is gaining formal qualifications in the management of risk. There are two qualifications for M_o_R Examinations, the Foundation and the Practitioner:

- **Foundation** – a multiple-choice paper consisting of 50 questions to be answered in 40 minutes. This is a closed-book examination.
- **Practitioner** – a case study question to test comprehension of the method, to be answered in three hours. Paper-based reference material can be used during this examination. Pre-reading material is issued just before the exam, and candidates are given 30 minutes reading time before the paper begins.

Accredited consulting and training organizations can help you gain accreditation. For more information on these, and the examinations for M_o_R, please visit the M_o_R website (www.m-o-r.org).

Accredited Consulting Organizations

Finding an ACO

Accredited Consulting Organizations (ACOs) employ experienced consultants who have been assessed on their knowledge of M_o_R, and have been recommended by the APM Group and OGC to provide advice on implementing M_o_R. Such consultants are known as M_o_R Registered Consultants. ACOs must also have undergone a full assessment by the APM Group of their organization's management systems and processes for undertaking consultancy assignments.

Eligibility of an ACO

To be eligible for certification as an ACO, an organization must meet, and continue to meet, the following criteria:

■ Have run at least one consultancy assignment within the 12 months prior to the date of application. For organizations that have been trading for less than two years, at least one director or senior employee must have run three or more consultancy assignments within the previous 36 months.

■ At all times, have only Registered Consultants leading any M_o_R assignment. Non-registered consultants can assist Registered Consultants to deliver consulting assignments.

■ At all times, have at least one consultant meeting the eligibility criteria for approved status as described below.

Assessment of M_o_R Registered Consultants

An M_o_R Registered Consultant will need to:

■ Have two years' experience in management consultancy services in general and two years' experience in the M_o_R method in particular

■ Demonstrate knowledge of M_o_R by having a high pass mark on the M_o_R Practitioner exam

■ Be able to provide four valid professional referees

■ Be able to present full oral evidence of at least one completed management consultancy assignment

■ Be able to present full oral evidence of at least one completed M_o_R consultancy assignment

■ Be able to provide a portfolio of evidence to show that the required standards can be met

■ Promote a professional image, particularly when presenting ideas and findings to a client.

ACO listing

A list of ACOs can be found on the APM Group website: www.m-o-r.org

Accredited Training Organizations

Eligibility of an ATO

APMG will assess organizations' course material and administration and management procedures. Accredited Training Organizations (ATOs) can either develop their own training material or license material from another ATO.

The following management and administration processes are also assessed as part of ATO accreditation:

- Organization management structure
- Organization quality control system including management review, internal audit, appeals and complaints procedures
- Course quality control system including delegate acceptance criteria (M_o_R)
- Course enrolment system (M_o_R)
- Pre-course documentation including joining instructions and pre-course reading material (M_o_R)
- The system for organization of the course venue including bookings, confirmation forms and procedures (M_o_R)
- Names and CVs of proposed trainers (M_o_R)
- Document control system
- Confidentiality waiver system (M_o_R)
- Training and competence of administration staff.

Assessment of an M_o_R trainer

The M_o_R trainer assessment will take place in two stages:

- Observation of the applicant presenting a number of M_o_R training sessions to students, preferably as part of a normal training course. This will be matched to the ATO material for those sessions and the M_o_R syllabus.
- Private assessment of the applicant's understanding of M_o_R methodology and applicability, in particular of those areas not covered by the presentation sessions.

ATO listing

A list of ATOs can be found on the APM Group website: www.m-o-r.org

Glossary

Acronyms

ACO	Accredited Consulting Organization
ATO	Accredited Training Organization
CCTA	Central Computer and Telecommunications Agency, one of the organizations that was merged to form the OGC
CRAMM	CCTA Risk Analysis and Management Method
EFQM	European Foundation for Quality Management
EMV	Estimated monetary value
HSE	Health and Safety Executive
ILGRA	Interdepartmental Liaison Group for Risk Assessment, secretariat provided by HSE
IT	Information Technology
M_o_R®	Management of risk (the brand name for this guidance)
MSP	Managing Successful Programmes
NPV	Net Present Value
OGC	Office of Government Commerce, part of HM Treasury
PEST(LE)	Analysis of political, economic, social, technological (and sometimes includes legal, environmental) factors
PRINCE2™	The standard UK government method for project management that provides a process-based framework for setting up and controlling projects; the acronym stands for 'projects in controlled environments'
RACI-VS	Analysis of roles and responsibilities of stakeholders: Responsible, Accountable, Consulted, Informed (and sometimes includes Verifies, Signs-off)
SMART	A mnemonic used at the project objective setting stage. It is a way of evaluating whether the objectives that are being set are appropriate. Specific, Measurable, Achievable, Relevant, Time-framed
SRO	Senior Responsible Owner
SWOT	Analysis of strengths, weaknesses, opportunities and threats within the given situation

Definitions

Accounting Officer

A public sector role with personal responsibility for the propriety and regularity of the finances for which he or she is answerable; includes responsibility for governance issues, and custodianship of the management of risk and its adoption throughout the organization.

Benefits

The measurable improvement resulting from an outcome perceived as an advantage by one or more stakeholders.

Business Case

The justification for an organizational activity [Strategic, Programme, Project, Operational] which typically contains costs, benefits, risks and timescales, and against which continuing viability is tested.

Business risk

Failure to achieve business objectives/benefits.

Communications Plan

A plan of the communications activities during the organizational activity [Strategic, Programme, Project or Operational]. Typically contains when, what, how and with whom information flows will be established and maintained.

Contingency planning

The process of identifying and planning appropriate responses to be taken when a risk actually occurs.

Corporate governance

The ongoing activity of maintaining a sound system of internal control by which the directors and officers of an organization ensure that effective management systems, including financial monitoring and control systems, have been put in place to protect assets, earning capacity and the reputation of the organization.

Dis-benefit

Outcomes perceived as negative by one or more stakeholders. Dis-benefits are actual consequences of an activity whereas, by definition, a risk has some uncertainty about whether it will materialize.

Enhancement

A risk response for an opportunity. Enhancement of an opportunity refers to both the realization of an opportunity and achieving additional gains over and above the opportunity.

Expected Value

This is calculated by multiplying the average impact by the probability percentage.

Exploitation

A risk response for an opportunity. Exploitation refers to changing an activity's scope, suppliers or specification in order to achieve a beneficial outcome.

Impact

Impact is the result of a particular threat or opportunity actually occurring.

Inherent risk

The exposure arising from a specific risk before any action has been taken to manage it.

Issue

A relevant event that has happened, was not planned and requires management action. Could be a problem, query, concern, change request or risk that has occurred.

Management of risk

See Risk management.

Management of risk framework

Sets the context within which risks are managed, in terms of how they will be identified, assessed and controlled. It must be consistent and comprehensive, with processes that are embedded in management activities throughout the organization.

Maturity level

A well-defined evolutionary plateau towards achieving a mature process (five levels are often cited: initial, repeatable, defined, managed and optimizing).

OGC Gateway™ Review

The OGC Gateway Review is a review of a delivery programme or procurement project carried out at a key decision point by a team of experienced people, independent of the project team.

Operational risk

Failure to achieve business/organizational objectives due to human error, system failures and inadequate procedure and controls.

Opportunity

An uncertain event that could have a favourable impact on objectives or benefits.

Outcome

The result of change, normally affecting real-world behaviour and/or circumstances. Outcomes are desired when a change is conceived. Outcomes are achieved as a result of the activities undertaken to effect the change. In a programme, the outcome is the manifestation of part or all of the new state conceived in the Blueprint.

Output

The tangible or intangible product resulting from a planned activity.

Probability

This is the evaluated likelihood of a particular threat or opportunity actually happening, including a consideration of the frequency with which this may arise.

Product

An input or output, whether tangible or intangible, that can be described in advance, created and tested. Also known as an output or deliverable.

Programme

Temporary flexible organization structure created to coordinate, direct and oversee the implementation of a set of related projects and activities in order to deliver outcomes and benefits related to the organization's strategic objectives. A programme is likely to have a life that spans several years.

Programme risk

Risk concerned with transforming high-level strategy into new ways of working to deliver benefits to the organization.

Project

A temporary organization that is created for the purpose of delivering one or more business products according to a specified Business Case.

Project risk

> Project risks are those concerned with the successful completion of the project. Typically these risks include personal, technical, cost, schedule, resource, operational support, quality and supplier issues.

Proximity (of risk)

> The time factor of risk, i.e. the occurrence of risks will be due at particular times, and the severity of their impact will vary depending on when they occur.

Realization

> A risk response for an opportunity. The realization of opportunities ensures that potential improvements to an organizational activity are delivered.

Reduction

> A risk response for a threat. Proactive actions are taken to reduce:
> - The probability of the event occurring by performing some form of control or
> - The impact of the threat should it occur.

Removal

> A risk response for a threat. Typically involves changing some aspect of the organizational activity, i.e. changing the scope, procurement route, supplier or sequence of activities.

Residual risk

> The risk remaining after the risk response has been applied.

Retention

> A risk response for a threat. A conscious and deliberate decision is taken to retain the threat, having discerned that it is more economical to do so than to attempt a Risk Response Action. The threat should continue to be monitored to ensure that it remains tolerable.

Risk

> An uncertain event or set of events that, should it occur, will have an effect on the achievement of objectives. A risk is measured by a combination of the probability of a perceived threat or opportunity occurring and the magnitude of its impact on objectives.

Risk Actionee

Some actions may not be within the remit of the Risk Owner to control explicitly; in that situation there should be a nominated owner of the action to address the risk. He or she will need to keep the Risk Owner apprised of the situation.

Risk appetite

An organization's unique attitude towards risk taking that in turn dictates the amount of risk that it considers is acceptable.

Risk cause

A description of the source of the risk, i.e. the event or situation that gives rise to the risk.

Risk Committee

A body of independent directors that is responsible for reviewing the company's internal control and risk management systems.

Risk effect

A description of the impact that the risk would have on the organizational activity should the risk materialize.

Risk estimation

The estimation of probability and impact of an individual risk, taking into account predetermined standards, target risk levels, interdependencies and other relevant factors.

Risk evaluation

The process of understanding the net effect of the identified threats and opportunities on an activity when aggregated together.

Risk event

A description of the area of uncertainty in terms of the threat or the opportunity.

Risk identification

Determination of what could pose a risk; a process to describe and list sources of risk (threats and opportunities).

Risk Log

See Risk Register.

Risk management

The systematic application of principles, approach and processes to the tasks of identifying and assessing risks, and then planning and implementing risk responses.

Risk Management Strategy

Describes the goals of applying risk management to the activity, a description of the process that will be adopted, the roles and responsibilities, risk thresholds, the timing of risk management interventions, the deliverables, the tools and techniques that will be used and reporting requirements. It may also describe how the process will be coordinated with other management activities.

Risk Management Policy

A high-level statement showing how risk management will be handled throughout the organization.

Risk Management Process Guide

Describes the series of steps (from Context through to Implement) and their respective associated activities, necessary to implement risk management.

Risk Manager

A role or individual responsible for the implementation of risk management for each activity at each of the organizational levels.

Risk Owner

A role or individual responsible for the management and control of all aspects of individual risks, including the implementation of the measures taken in respect of each risk.

Risk perception

The way in which a stakeholder views a risk, based on a set of values or concerns.

Risk Profile

Describes the types of risk that are faced by an organization and its exposure to those risks.

Risk Register

A record of identified risks relating to an initiative, including their status and history.

Risk response

Actions that may be taken to bring the situation to a level where the exposure to risk is acceptable to an organization. These responses fall into one of a number of risk response categories.

Risk response category

For threats, the individual risk response category can be reduction, removal, transfer, retention or share of one or more risks. For opportunities, the individual risk response category can be realization, enhancement or exploitation or share of one or more risks.

Risk tolerance

The threshold levels of risk exposure, which with appropriate approvals can be exceeded, but which when exceeded will trigger some form of response (e.g. reporting the situation to senior management for action).

Risk tolerance line

A line drawn on the Summary Risk Profile. Risks that appear above this line cannot be accepted (lived with) without referring them to a higher authority. For a project, the Project Manager would refer these risks to the Senior Responsible Owner.

Senior Responsible Owner

The single individual with overall responsibility for ensuring that a project or programme meets its objectives and delivers the projected benefits.

Severity of risk

The degree to which the risk could affect the situation.

Share

A risk response for a threat. Modern procurement methods commonly entail a form of risk sharing through the application of a pain/gain formula: both parties share the gain (within pre-agreed limits) if the cost is less than the cost plan; and share the pain (again within pre-agreed limits) if the cost plan is exceeded.

Sponsor

The main driving force behind a programme or project.

Stakeholder

Any individual, group or organization that can affect, be affected by, or perceives itself to be affected by, an initiative [programme, project, activity, risk].

Strategic risk

Risk concerned with where the organization wants to go, how it plans to get there, and how it can ensure survival.

Summary Risk Profile

A simple mechanism to increase visibility of risks. It is a graphical representation of information normally found on an existing Risk Register.

Threat

An uncertain event which could have a negative impact on objectives or benefits.

Transfer

A risk response for a threat, whereby a third party takes on responsibility for an aspect of the threat.

Index

Index